Problem Solving

*Simple tools and techniques
which everyone can understand*

Jitendra M. Pant

Copyright © All rights reserved

No part of this book may be reproduced, transmitted, or stored in a retrieval system, in any form or by any means, electronic, mechanical, photocopying, or otherwise, without the permission of the author.

Dedicated to my parents
Late Shri Lalit Mohan Pant and
Late Smt Mohini Pant

And my eldest brother
Late Shri Krishna Mohan Pant

Contents

		Page no.
	Acknowledgement	ix
	Preface	xi
	Understanding Problem	1
1	What is a Problem?	2
2	Problem Solving Steps	11
3	Identification of Problem	18
4	Selection of Problem	23
5	Define Problem	25
	Measure	30
6	Measurement and Data Collection	31
	Analyse	35
7	Check sheet	36
8	Histogram	39
9	Graphs	45
10	Scatter Diagram	48
11	Pareto Analysis	50
12	Fish Bone Diagram	54
13	5W1H analysis	59
14	Why….Why Analysis	64
15	FMEA Analysis	68
16	Force Field Analysis	75
17	Gantt Chart	80

Analyse-continued

18	Process Mapping	82
19	Control Charts	86
20	Affinity Diagram	90
21	Interrelationship (Relations) Diagram	93
22	Tree Diagram	97
23	Matrix Diagram	99
24	Arrow Diagram	101
25	Process Decision Program Chart	103
26	Mind Mapping	106
27	Benchmarking	108
28	Data Analysis-few more tools	111

Improve — 119

29	Six Thinking Hats	120
30	Poka Yoke	125
31	Lateral Thinking	132
32	SCAMPER	137
33	Brainstorming	142
34	TRIZ	146
35	Kaizen	163

Control — 166

36	Standardise	167
37	Control sheets / Check sheets	172

More Problem-Solving Approaches — 174

38	Theory of Constraints	175
39	Business Process Reengineering	179
40	Six Sigma	189
41	Process Capability Studies	194
42	Lean Management	198
43	JIT	201
44	Kanban	205
45	TPM	209

Decision Making And Implementation — 217

46	Decision Making	218
47	Evaluating Solutions	221
48	Implementation	225

Problem Solving Competencies — 227

49	Holistic Thinking	228
50	Competencies	231

Bibliography	236
About J.M.Pant	238

"If I had an hour to solve a problem I'd spend 55 minutes thinking about the problem and 5 minutes thinking about solutions." ....

Albert Einstein

"We always hope for the easy fix: the one simple change that will erase a problem in a stroke. But few things in life work this way. Instead, success requires making a hundred small steps go right - one after the other, no slipups, no goofs, everyone pitching in."
— **Atul Gawande,** American surgeon and author, from his second book **Better: A Surgeon's Notes on Performance.**

Acknowledgement

The encouragement and inspiration to write is from my family-my wife Sunita, my children Kushagra and Prerna, and their spouse Shilpa and Paritosh. My grandchildren Siddharth and Khushi are the driving force, and I have seen in my 3-year-old Siddharth the power of observation and the questioning way of problem solving like Toyota's Why..Why technique and Socrates questioning style.

One can draw valuable lessons on problem solving by observing children's behaviour when faced with a problem. What I have found with Siddharth is that he will not be satisfied by doing a task once. He will repeat it and do it in different ways. Probably this is what we mean by generating several alternatives and not rest with one solution, which may not be the best. Repetition ensures that the solution works on all occasions. Children are believed to have a hundred different ways of thinking, of discovering and learning, and can express themselves through painting, drawing, dance, modelling, imaginative play, song creation and friendship.

I am always inspired by my elder brother Madan, a walking encyclopaedia on most subjects, who strongly recommends putting down one's work in book form.

I am indebted to organisations, in India and overseas, who have given me opportunities through various assignments, and from where I have gained a rich experience in problem solving. The approach and techniques of Problem Solving are used while aiming at Operations Excellence through 5S, Kaizen, TPM, TQM, Six Sigma, Lean management, BPR, Quality circles, and so forth. Some of these organisations are Sunflag Iron & Steel Ltd, Orient Bell Ltd, Motherson Sumi, Dabur Ltd, Hindustan Unilever, NTPC, GAIL, Adani Mundra port, Wolkem, Macrographics, Doshi Ion, Hero Honda, L&T, HP, Aptech, Tata Infotech (now part of TCS), Maruti, Tata Motors, FAAAI/AOTS, Escorts, JK Tyres, Bajaj Auto, BEC Fertilisers, Chambal Fertilisers, BEC Engineering, Indraprastha Gas and Khandelwal Cables.

20 Oct 2018　　　　　　　　　　Jitendra M Pant
New Delhi

Preface

Increasingly organisations are looking at problem solving as a critical competency in potential leaders. The ability to formulate a problem and think out solutions will remain useful even in the times of artificial intelligence, big data analytics, machine learning and robotics. The aim of the book is to improve one's ability to solve problems collaboratively and provides tools and templates that support problem solving.

What is a problem today, becomes a golden opportunity tomorrow. Till the utility is discovered, every weed and every rock is a nuisance, making the soil infertile. As the solutions to these problems are found, the weed becomes a useful plant for food and medicinal requirement, and the rock is a useful mineral like bauxite, iron ore, limestone etc. Solutions to problems endows economic value and generates opportunities to create wealth, better health and improves quality of life.

Entrepreneurs are made because they identify problems and find a business opportunity through solution to the problems. Transport difficulties and inconvenience gave rise to Uber and Ola cabs; poor quality water to mineral water plants; mosquito repellents of various types are in the market because of mosquito menace. Entrepreneurs spot problems and convert them into business ventures; other folks only lament and discuss the problems but are not able to formulate the problem, identify its root cause and think creatively a solution to overcome the problem.

Are problems good or bad? Not being able to identify problems is bad. The culture must be conducive to problem solving-people should be encouraged and praised when they recognise problems. More the problems, bigger is the opportunity for improvement and progress. Burying our heads in sand like ostrich, hoping the problem will fade away, is a defeating approach. If a person says there are no problems in his work place or organisation, then that is a problem! 'No problem' is a problem.

20 October 2018   Jitendra M. Pant
New Delhi

Understanding Problem

1
What Is A Problem?

"We cannot solve our problems with the same level of thinking that created them." …Albert Einstein.

The first and most crucial step in problem solving is being able to understand the problem you wish to solve. Often, we mistake the symptoms for the problem. For example, you are having 100-degree F fever. Is fever the problem? If the doctor diagnoses the cause as malaria, is malaria the real problem? Or the stagnant water left in coolers, allowing mosquitoes to grow, is the real problem?

I have been suffering from foot numbness, heaviness in legs and mobility problem for few years. The doctor diagnosed it as venous insufficiency and I got my leg operated for varicose vein. The situation did not improve. It appears the real cause is nerve related and problem is neurogenic claudication for which the solutions and treatment are totally different though the symptoms are similar. Even the best doctors make mistakes in understanding what the problem is. Symptom was same, but causes were different.

Problem is the obstacle, constraint or an issue which prevents us or makes it difficult to achieve the desired goal.

Problem is the gap between what is happening at present and what is expected and desired.

Problem and opportunity are two sides of the same coin. Problems can be viewed as opportunities to improve.

Space problem in warehouse results in demand for another storage area. Is space the problem? Why is the finished goods inventory piling up? Why are there huge stocks of non-moving inventory lying in warehouse? Why are goods stored in warehouse which have been returned by the customer? Why is the vertical space in warehouse not utilised? Asking such questions will show where the real problem is. Without such understanding of problem, the solutions will be disastrous.

Symptom is the evidence, quantitative or qualitative, that indicates the existence of a disturbance or disorder related to any process. Space shortage is the symptom in above example.

Cause is the reason for a condition, situation or action. Cause brings about an effect or result. There may be many causes for a problem and identifying the root cause is one major competency in problem solving.

Exploring the Problem
Asking few questions (the Socrates method) will help in exploring and understanding the scope of the problem.

Who – is the person or group of persons that could be a cause of the problem. Is it because of lack of skill, willingness, fitness, or lack of inner drive.

Where - the place where work is being done, or the situation is occurring. Is place the problem? Is there a need to change? Outsource work? Or Insource work?

What – the purpose of what is being done? Is the purpose ambiguous, confused? Can it be redefined? Can it be eliminated? Does it need further working? Is lack of clarity of purpose the problem?

When - is the time of working, studying or sleeping the problem area? Are defects happening in a specific shift? Are you having insufficient sleep? Are working hours too strenuous?

Why - asking why can help in clearer understanding of the problem and working out causes. Why is the house electricity bill high? Why one is not able to reach office on time? Why one keeps falling sick?

How – the process, the method or way of doing things can be the problem. 'It is done this way, always' is the pet reply. But if we keep doing things the way they were being done before, there will be no improvement and the problem will not go. Problems will not disappear on their own.

Putting problems into solvable form

Imagine you have been given the task of improving the efficiency of your company's accounting procedures. Numerous questions come to mind, for instance, what does efficiency mean, exactly what procedures need to be made more efficient, what are the problems with these procedures, do the company's training programs need to be improved, what about office automation?

Most problems are amorphous and complex. We must create order out of chaos. Before we can find a solution, we must define the problem, identify its cause and effect relationships, and put it into solvable form.

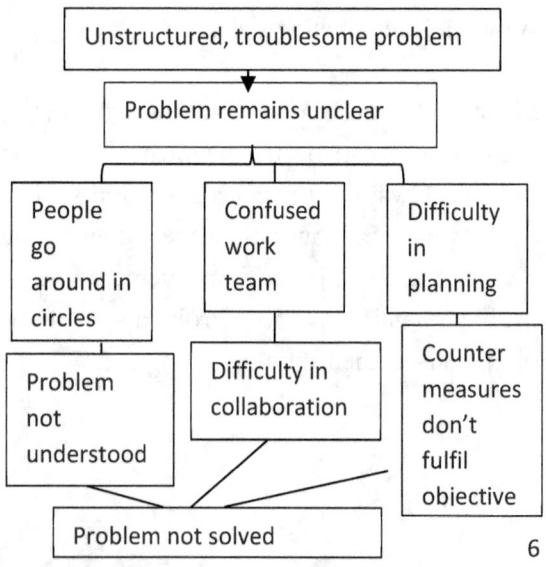

<Problems put in solvable form>

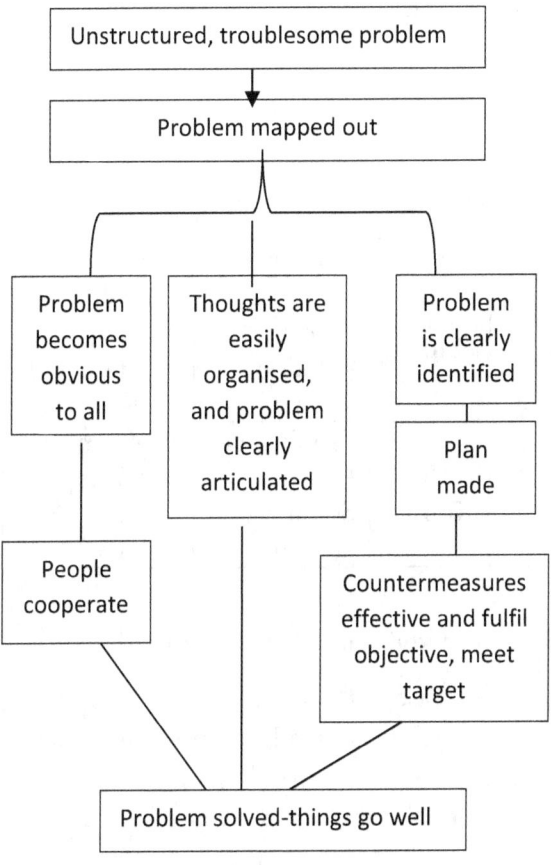

There may be many types of problems, personal life related and work related. From problem solving point of view, they can be put in a matrix.

		Solution	
		Known	Not Known
Problem	**Known**	Problem known, Solution known	Problem known, Solution not known
	Not Known	Problem not known, Solution known	Problem not known, Solution not known

Problem known, Solution known

In most cases of breakdowns and stoppages, the problem is known like worn out gasket or washer, sensor not working and so forth, and the solutions to fix them are also known.

Problem known, Solution not known

In above case, why does the problem keep repeating and why are the stoppages not reducing to zero is a more chronic problem for which the solutions are not easily available.

Problem not known, Solution known

Here the difficulty lies in identifying problem and catching the culprit, that is the root cause of the problem, as the root cause may be hidden among many layers of superficial manifestations of problem.

In a textile plant making white cloth, in the evening around dusk, a coloured streak was coming in cloth making it unfit for use and a big loss to the company. The problem would disappear during day hours. A closer, round the clock study for a week, revealed that during evening hours, mosquitoes would sit on the hot rolls of calendaring machine and get crushed in the process, leaving a coloured streak on the cloth. Once the cause was known, the solution to get rid of mosquitoes in the work area was easier.

Problem not known, Solution not known

Such cases require collaboration, calling of experts and outside help of people who have experienced such problems and have successfully worked on their solutions.

In some cases, it remains unresolved till technological and scientific innovations provide an answer.

How good are you at problem solving?

		1	2	3	4
1	I focus on running current operations smoothly				
2	I generate multiple solutions to a problem				
3	I develop implementation plan for my solution				
4	I define problem before analysing and solving it				
5	I go by intuition rather than facts and data which are cumbersome to gather				
6	I work on big problems as small problems do not give benefits				
7	I ask questions at each stage of problem solving				
8	I do not consult others during problem solving				
9	I can solve problems through observation				
10	I avoid problems				

Scale:
1.Always; 2. Often; 3. Sometimes; 4. Not at all

2
Problem Solving Steps

Though problems sometimes can be solved by intuition, in most cases the flash in the pan insight fails. The Eureka moment comes to those who have been thinking over the problem for days. A structured way of problem solving increases the success rate.

Problem Solving Steps (QC circles approach)

Step 1: Identification of Problem
Step 2: Selection of Problem
Step 3: Define the Problem
Step 4: Measurement and Data Collection
Step 5: Analysis of the Problem
Step 6: Finding the Root Cause
Step 7: Improve-Develop Solutions
Step 8: Foreseeing problems and working out countermeasures
Step 9: Trial implementation and check
Step 10: Regular Implementation
Step 11: Control Measures
Step 12: Evaluate and Monitor

Problem solving steps- The Toyota approach:

1. Clarify the problem. Decide why it is a problem. Determine the benefits of solving the problem. Consider how it fits into the business and the effects it will have on current goals. GO SEE the problem first hand. GEMBA Walk (Gemba-work place).
2. Break down the problem into smaller problems. GO SEE each small problem. Study inputs and outputs of the process. Prioritise.
3. Set the target, time lines
4. Analyse the root cause. Identify factors and address all potential root causes. GO and SEE root causes. Validate.
5. Develop countermeasures to remove root cause. Develop as many alternatives as possible. Narrow down to most practical and effective.
6. Implement countermeasures.
7. Monitor results and Process.
8. Standardise and share success.

The approach gives importance to going to the work area where action is and using the senses of seeing, hearing, touching, smelling, to understand the situation.

Problem solving the Six Sigma way:
The five key steps (DMAIC as an acronym) are:
1. Define
2. Measure
3. Analyse
4. Improve
5. Control

Kaizen approach-PDCA

Kaizen or continuous improvement is done by following the PDCA cycle, and Standardising. The next level of improvement is improving on the past standard by repeating PDCA. The continuous rotation of PDCA leads to progress of business, society, individual and the nation.

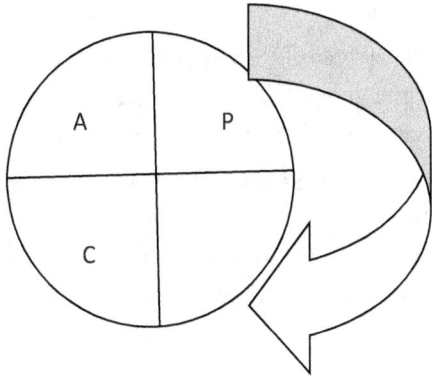

P: Plan

What is to be done?
How it is to be done? When? Who will do?

D: Do

Implement the planned solution

C: Check

Check whether what was achieved was as per plan. Use reliable measurement techniques.

D: Action

If there are gaps between actual and plan, improve the way of doing things so that the planned target is realised. If plan is deficient, revise the plan.

All approaches say almost the same thing. Some have 12 points, others 8, 5 or 4. It is a matter of elaboration. I have mentioned them here together so that one can draw learnings from each and formulate one's own problem-solving methodology which is suitable for his or her work and services.

Bad planning increases time for checking and corrective action –the overall time taken to solve the problem increases dramatically

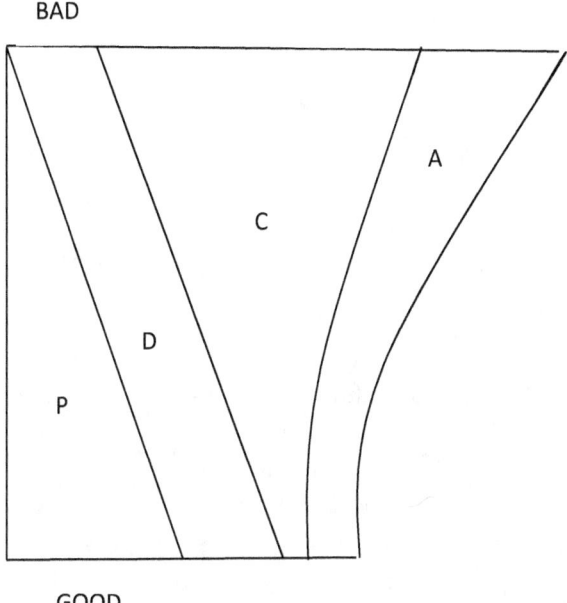

More time should be spent on Planning and Execution, so that time spent on checking and action is reduced.

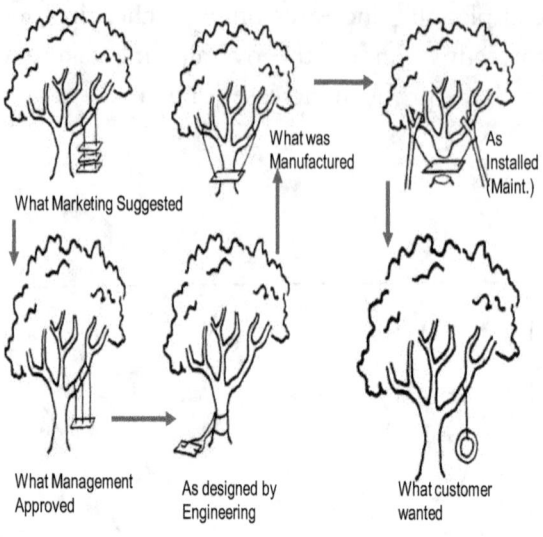

Above is an example of an ill-defined problem.

"The formulation of the problem is often more essential than its solution, which may be merely a matter of mathematical or experimental skill."
— **Albert Einstein**

Problem solving in groups

	Known to Self	Unknown to Self
Known to Others	A	B
Unknown to others	C	D

(Johari Window)

The first group session will extract people's current thoughts about the problem- square A.

A single individual or department possesses the knowledge represented by squares A and C only. Trying to solve problems alone is not very effective.

When others join in, the knowledge represented by square B is added.

With repeated use of problem solving techniques, the group begins to generate ideas and starts to develop the knowledge represented by square D. It is important to keep on trying.

3
Identification of Problem

Problems are the keys to hidden treasure. The more problems one can identify, greater will be the opportunity to improve, to make wealth, to have better health, to learn, to reduce cost, to increase speed, to raise quality, productivity and safety standards.

A problem exists only if there is a difference between what is happening and what you desire to be happening.

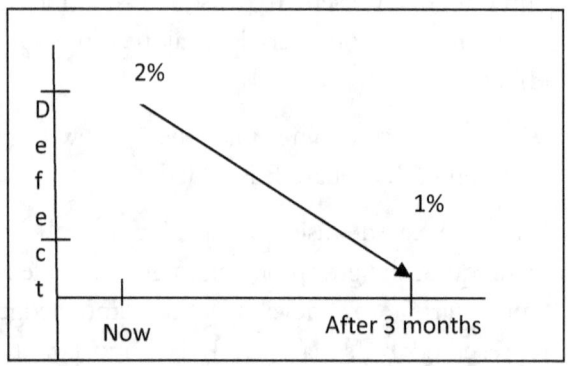

As the graph shows, the current level of defects is 2% and the desire is to bring it down to 1% in three months. This is the correct way of defining a problem-the present status, the desired status and the period in which the problem resolution is needed.

If the time frame is missing, the problem is ill defined as one does not know when the problem will be resolved. If the existing level and the targeted level are not known, one cannot gauge whether the improvement has been made.

It is evident that measure is needed to understand the problem. What cannot be measured cannot be improved upon.

How to identify problems?

1. Performance gaps. Is there a gap in expected performance and actual performance? Is performance variation large; that is the performance is excellent one day and dismal after few days-there are many peaks and valleys. Are there concerns in performance related to low productivity, equipment breakdowns and minor stoppages, poor quality, high cost, safety incidents (accidents) on the rise?
2. Customer dissatisfaction. Are complaints increasing? Is the expense on customer warranty claims on the rise? Are we not getting repeat

customers? Is market share falling? Are customers returning goods because of problems?
3. Delivery delayed. Is there delay in delivery promised to the client?
4. Payables: Are suppliers, employees, contractors, logistic providers not being paid on time?
5. Receivables: Are overdues mounting?
6. Inventory: Is inventory of finished goods beyond norms? Are there non-moving inventories?
7. Is cleanliness, orderliness and maintenance below par?
8. Is my weight reducing without any efforts on my part? Is my weight increasing though my diet is in control? Is my blood pressure varying from low to high during the day?

Following techniques can be used for identifying problems:
- Brainstorming: This unlocks the creative power of the group. The topic of brainstorming must be stated precisely. Quantity is important, not quality, as analysis, evaluation and criticism of ideas is done later. Ideas should flow freely.

- Observation-go to the work place, see the actual work, actually. Japanese call it Genchi, Genbutsu, Genjitsu.
- Data analysis-data of quality, safety, breakdowns, abnormalities, cost, inventory, production, services, health data, financial data, etc.
- Voice of customer through customer feedback and complaints, solicited and unsolicited.
- Budget versus actual analysis, KPI (key performance indicator) analysis, and identifying gaps.
- Feedback from stakeholders (customers, suppliers, employees, investors, collaborators, dealers, partners, society), top management.
- Benchmarking internally or with other organisations better than one's own.

Problem Identification Matrix

A simple matrix for identifying the problem and its source, particularly useful when one needs to focus to find out what is the real problem to be solved.

	People	Process	System
Mystery Something is wrong but not clear why			
Opportunity There are benefits and advantages to be gained			
Puzzle Complex challenge			
Difficulty Not knowing how to realise the goal			
Dilemma What choices to make?			
Who?			
What?			
Where?			
When?			
Why?			

4
Selection of Problem

All problems cannot be resolved at one go. One needs to prioritise so that the important problems are tackled first.

The rules of priority must be framed by the person responsible for solving problems. Pareto principle or 80:20 rule can be used for prioritisation.

A large problem should be broken down into biteable, small sized problems, so that it can be solved and implemented in short period (say one to three months). The achievement in problem solving motivates the doer and the people around.

Do not select 'world hunger projects' which are too ambitious and will take years to accomplish. Problems which take too long a time to resolve affect the morale of the team and interest on the project dwindles. The top management also loses interest and the project gets abandoned. Small victories in accomplishing projects is the best way to continue moving forward.

Aids for prioritising problem for selection:
- Use Pareto analysis based on quantitative data or ranking method. Categorise into A, B and C type problems. Prioritise based on the criticality, benefits and impact.
- Repetitive failures like accidents, customer complaints, wrong billing, missing delivery dates, repetitive rejections, repetitive breakdowns, traffic jams, pollution, illness, farmer suicides, lack of jobs, school dropout rate, malnutrition, and so forth.
- Prioritisation based on Benefits versus Cost analysis
- Break large project into smaller projects with completion time of 1 to 3 months; celebrate small victories.
- Problems seen from an outsider's perspective-feedback from customers, suppliers, employees, shareholders, bankers, investors, society, visitors, callers on phone or social media.

5
Define Problem

A well-defined problem enables good analysis and ensures that the solution found will be for the defined problem and not something else.

Problem Statement
- Describe and Define current situation with facts and data. Be specific. One should have metrics and method/instrument/gauge to measure. For qualitative items, use a ranking scale method.
- Identify stakeholders using RACI (Responsible, Accountable, Consulted and Informed).
- Define desired situation.
- Set target objectives for the desired situation. This should be measurable.
- Set time line for resolution of the problem.
- Create a problem statement after discussing with stakeholders. All should be having the same understanding. The criteria for success and what will be achieved after solving

the problem (like impact on business) must be clear to all.

While defining problem, following tools and measurements can be used:
1. Process flow chart
2. Sketch-product, equipment, process
3. Layout diagram
4. Time studies, capacity studies
5. Before/After scenario
6. Process capability studies with measures of Cp, Cpk
7. OEE index (Overall equipment effectiveness).
8. COPQ (Cost of Poor Quality), COQ (Cost of Quality).

Enablers: are the drivers, the facilitators, the experts, the consultants and external collaborators that provide support for transition from current state to the desired state.

Barriers: are the roadblocks, constraints, obstacles that will prevent resolution of the problem. The biggest barrier is the mindset which resists change. While making the transition, opposition will come as follows:
'This will not work…it is not practical.'

'We tried in the past and it failed.'

'I have 30 years of experience and you are telling me that my process is wrong.'

Template-Problem Statement

CURRENT STATE	GAP	DESIRED STATE
Where are we now?		Where do we want to be?

PROBLEM STATEMENT
Our current defect level is 2% and we want to reduce it to 1% in three months' time. The gap of 1% defect is the problem we must resolve within 3 months.

Stakeholder Name:		
R: Responsible		
A: Accountable		
C: Consulted		
I: Informed		

> The causal relationship, as seen in the next diagram, may show many likely causes. One must validate the active causes for the problem being tackled. The root cause must be traced.

Problem and its probable causes

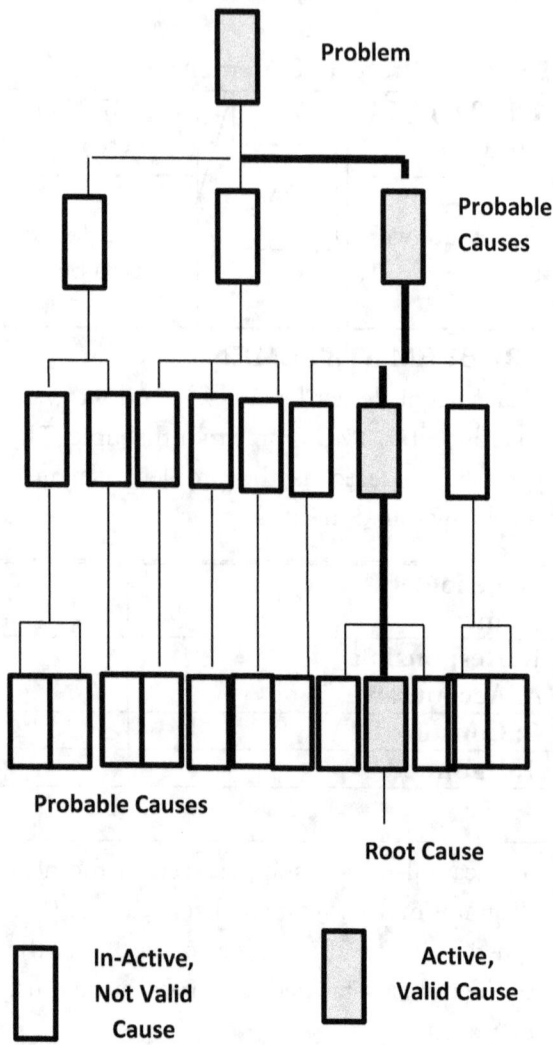

Mini Case

A food product manufacturing company has a dust free packing line with metal detectors, just before packing, so that if any micron size particle is detected, the packing is not done. The room is humidity and temperature controlled. The operators work with gloves and head gear and pass through an air shower before entering the packing line room. Company has made good investment in this room. Production output is an all-time high with plant working three shifts (24 hours a day) but customer complaints of metallic particles in the product has not reduced from its average level of 5 complaints per month. In fact, one customer lost his teeth after biting the food product and has sued the company for damages. CEO wants to improve the situation in one month.

1. What is the current situation?
2. What is the desired situation?
3. What is the nature of the problem?
4. Who is affected? What is the impact?
5. Where is the problem happening?
6. When is the problem happening?
7. Construct the problem statement.

Measure

6

Measurement and Data Collection

Problem should be understood based on facts and data. What cannot be measured cannot be controlled, managed or improved. We cannot focus on what we do not measure.

One caution. In the book on Statistics for Management by Levin and Rubin, there is a quote of Benjamin Disraeli: 'There are three kinds of lies: lies, damned lies and Statistics.'

Though data is extremely important for problem solving, unfortunately on most occasions, measurement and data itself is the problem. If a weighing machine is not calibrated at timely intervals using standard weights, we may be measuring weight, but it could be either under or overweight. You must have seen weighing bridges by the roadside called Dharam Kaanta (Hindi word meaning legitimate weigh bridge). Trucks take weighment in these weigh bridges. Company has its own weigh bridge which shows a different reading. Then the client who receives the material has his own weighing system which gives another reading. Weighment itself has become a problem in this case. It leads to conflict, time wastage on meetings and reconciling different readings and trying to find out the real culprit. In the end the matter is settled through negotiation.

Let's take another situation. The company's MIS system shows defects are coming down in the plant. But a look at customer feedback reports show that customer returns are increasing. There is a likelihood that the internal quality data is manipulated.

Some organisations say they use SAP and data is computerised. The suggestion is that data cannot be tampered. Yes, the integrity of data can be ensured if the data is captured directly by the computer which happens in automated plants. But when data is entered manually on log book, some register, diary or piece of paper, there is a chance of transcription, data entry or even intentional error.

While doing measurement and data collection, ensure the following:

1. Source of data must be known and clearly defined.
2. Metrics are well defined.

3. The measurement method is clear.
4. The instruments and gauges are calibrated as per stipulated schedule.
5. Collection of past and current data.
6. Measurement of both average and variation (sigma). Averages are deceptive. Problems are generally hidden within variation. Most organisations (and even country's statistics) talk of averages, while the problem lies in variation. The per capita income may be high, but the gap in incomes of rich and poor could be a major problem.

   First reduce the variation, then take steps to improve the averages, and not the other way around.
7. Integrity of data
8. Validity and reliability of data
9. Automate to the extent possible
10. Managers must measure themselves on sample basis, and cross check data.

In operations, measures like Cp, Cpk (for process capability), COQ (Cost of Quality) and COPQ (Cost of Poor Quality), OEE (Overall Equipment Effectiveness) are useful. Finance uses measures of EBITDA (Earnings before interest, tax, depreciation and amortisation), ROI (return on investment) etc.

Data may be numerical and verbal. Most tools of problem solving are used for analysing numerical data. But facts cannot always be expressed by numerical data. People usually possess more verbal data than numerical data. For example, buyers of a washing machine may express their dissatisfaction through verbal statements like 'controls are badly positioned,' 'styling is old fashioned,' 'in single colour only,' 'not convenient to use,' and so forth.

As verbal data represents facts, both numerical and verbal data must be organized and used in problem solving. Numerical data is organized using histogram, scatter diagram, Pareto chart, graphs, control charts, fish bone, Gantt chart, and various statistical methods. Verbal data can be organized through mind maps, affinity diagram, relations diagram, tree diagram etc. which are referred in later chapters.

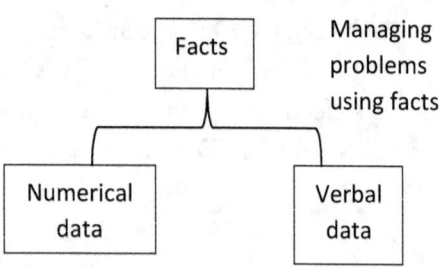

Managing problems using facts

Analyse

7
Check Sheet

Check sheet is designed for data collection for a specific problem. Check sheet could also be prepared for inspection, review, audit or monitoring.

You want to understand why you are not able to produce 100% defect free (diameter within tolerance) rounds after centerless grinding. For this study, first prepare a check sheet for a week's data on diameter as under:

Check sheet for defects- Centreless grinding			
	Diameter in mm		
Hour	Machine1	Machine 2	Machine 3
08:30 hrs			
09:30 hrs			
10:30 hrs			
11:30 hrs			
12:00 hrs			
13:00 hrs			
14:00 hrs			
15:00 hrs			
16:00 hrs			

The data will be used for finding the process capability of the process, machine and people, and will be subject to further analysis based on the current level of Cp and Cpk.

Examples of check sheet to understand purchase order errors, and defects in manufacturing, are shared below. Counting can be done using tally marks and crossing them after 5, so that counting becomes easy.

| Check sheet for errors-Purchase Orders ||||||
Errors	Jan	Feb	Mar	Apr	May
Wrong address					
Quantity					
Specifications					
Price					
Payment terms					
Delivery date					

Check sheet for defects-inspection

Product: Lot no	No.. inspected:	
Inspector's name	Date:	
Type of defect	Number of	Total
Cracks	⊞ ⊞⊞⊞⊞⊞	25
Scratch		50
Blowholes		75
Dimension		20
Surface finish		15
Others		15
		200

I am sharing an example of check sheet for inspection and monitoring of toilet cleanliness. You will see this in many malls and corporate offices of public and private sector.

Unfortunately, check sheets are not seen in plants and offices other than corporate. Or in shops other than malls.

Toilets and drinking water points are hygiene factors which should get the highest priority in any organisation. Once the toilets are built, maintenance of toilets in hygienic and clean condition is a problem. Check sheets for toilets will help in better understanding and keeping the toilets well maintained and clean.

Check sheet for Toilets

Check points	9am	11am	1pm	3pm	5pm
Wash basin					
Leaking tap					
Flush working					
Water supply					
Naphthalene balls					
Room freshener					
Overall cleanliness					
Signature of supervisor/ manager					
Date					

8
Histogram

Most of us would have studied histogram in school, and later in college. Histogram is a useful tool for analysing variation. The spread of data points around the mean gives useful insights about the process and its stability.

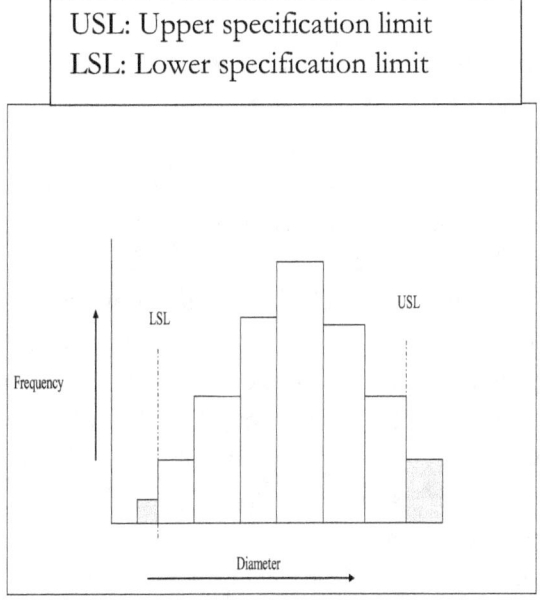

The customer provides the expected quality standards through these specifications. The range is the tolerance provided. In above histogram, few readings are in the shaded region outside specifications. Histogram is based on sample data, but from the above diagram, one can conclude that defects are being created in the process and unless 100% fool proof detection is done, defective products are likely to reach the customer.

The mean value may be well within the tolerance limits and the producer may be happy that he is producing quality products. He is shocked when he keeps receiving customer complaints and sees rework being done in the plant. Many meetings, shouting, firing people, and crisis is created but that is not going to solve the problem. Solution lies in cool thinking and analysis of causes of variation and reducing the variation. The measure of variation is sigma. What is implied is the need to first measure sigma and then analyse causes for high sigma. Finding solutions to these causes will help in reducing sigma. The smaller the sigma, better is the quality.

An example of skewed histogram is illustrated below.

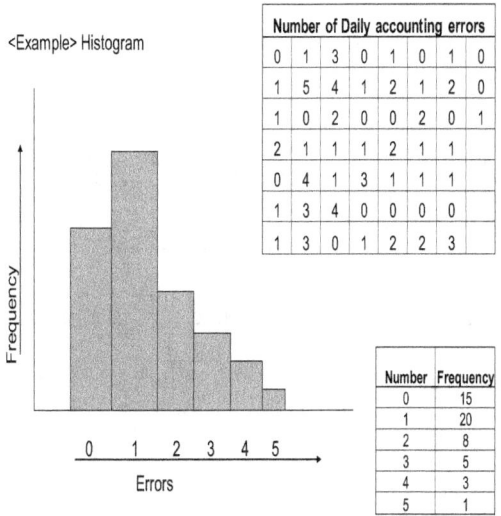

In cases like accounting errors, purchase order errors, customer complaints and customer returns, the target must be Zero.

In his book Jack: Straight from the gut, Jack Welch of GE fame, recalls an experience where his team was celebrating reduction of order to delivery cycle time from 16 days to 8 days, but Jack realised that his customers felt nothing except variance and unpredictability. Some customers got their orders 9 days late, while others got them 6 days early.

Customer expectation: 8-day order to delivery cycle

Existing process Delivery cycle days	After Improvement- cycle days
20	17
15	2
30	5
10	12
5	4
Average 16 days	Average 8 days

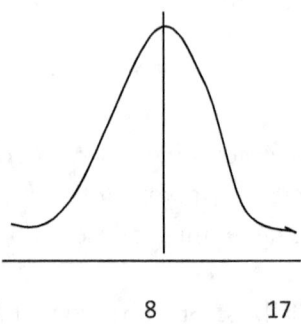

There was internal celebration because of big improvement from 16 days to 8 days (50% reduction), but customer feels frustrated with the 15-day span, unsure of what delivery he would get.

The key is to control the internal processes and reduce the variation, which in this case resulted in following outcome:

Existing process Delivery cycle days	After Improvement cycle days
20	7
15	9
30	9
10	8
5	7
Average 16 days	Average 8 days

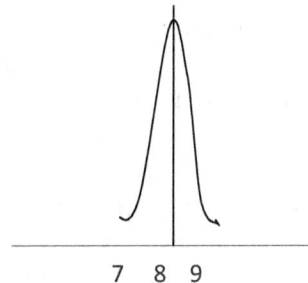

7   8   9

The improvement in average is same, but sigma is substantially reduced, and the span of variation is 2 days which creates customer delight.

An easy way of understanding variation is to keep your left foot in hot water at 50 deg C and right foot in ice water at 4 deg C. The average is 27 deg C which should feel nice. But do you feel that way!

Buy fast food- hot and nice today, lukewarm and insipid the next day. That's variation. Would you trust such a food outlet?

Arrival on airport- baggage claim: maybe 5 minutes, may be 20 minutes. Large variation! Would you be happy waiting for your baggage in such uncertain system.

Asking for home loan- bank says two to three weeks. That's variation. Will you trust such a bank? How can you plan your next steps for building your dream home?

Variance is sigma squared and adds up. If the parts in the chain, the supply network or any process, have variance, the total variance becomes extremely large. If the part made by you must fit into another part, variation can create havoc.

9
Graphs

Graphs are a good way of visualising data, seeing patterns, proportions and trends. Various types of graphs like line, bar, pie, radar, run chart can be used. Excel is very convenient for making graphs.

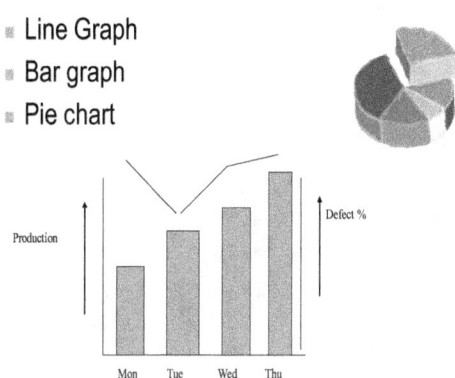

A **radar chart** shows multivariate data in the form of a two-dimensional chart of three or more quantitative variables represented on axes starting from the same point.

Radar Chart

Equipment	OEE %
CNC milling	86
Centreless grinding	80
Boring machine	75
Hardening furnace	70
Drawing machine	86
Shot blasting	80

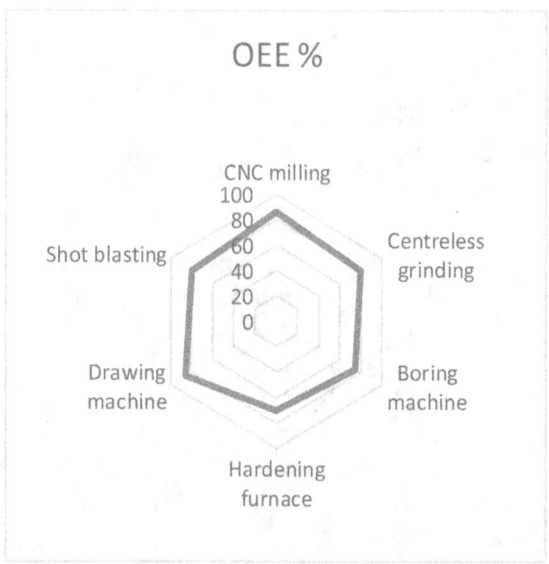

Run chart

A **run chart** is a line **graph** of data, like defects or specific quality characteristic, plotted over time. By collecting and charting data over time, one can find trends or patterns in the process, and facilitate analysis. Since they do not use control limits, **run charts** cannot tell whether process is stable. However, they can show you how the process is **running.**

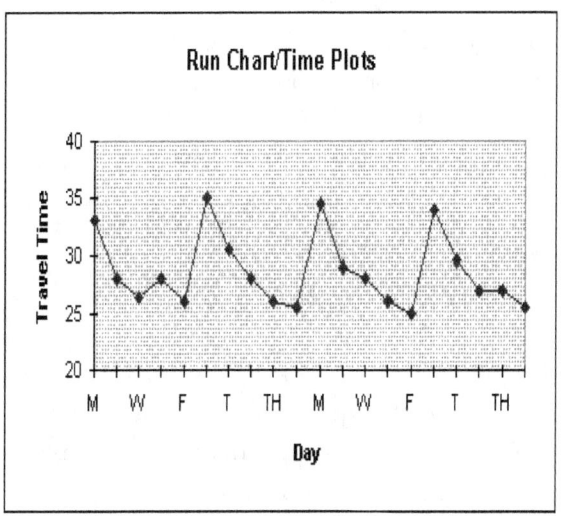

10
Scatter Diagram

Scatter diagrams help in understanding correlation between two variables, and thereby enable identification of the real cause of a problem.

The correlation coefficient can be computed statistically, and its value will lie between -1 and +1. The variables could show strong positive correlation, strong negative correlation or insignificant correlation.

Example of insignificant or zero correlation:
- Marks in examination versus height of students.
- Weight of a person and IQ level.

Examples of negative correlation
- Good quality percentage versus customer complaints (quality goes up, complaints come down).
- Heating cost versus temperature of room (lower is the room temperature, more will be the heating cost).

Examples of positive correlation
- Height versus weight.
- Overtime and excess working hours versus errors made.

Patterns of Scatter Diagram

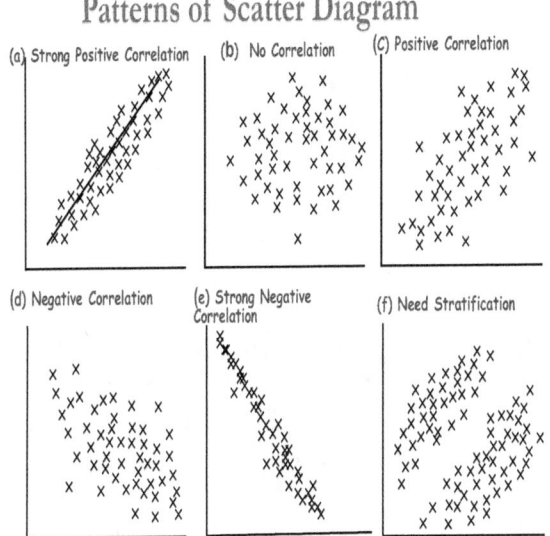

(a) Strong Positive Correlation
(b) No Correlation
(c) Positive Correlation
(d) Negative Correlation
(e) Strong Negative Correlation
(f) Need Stratification

11
Pareto Analysis

Pareto Analysis aids in prioritisation of problems during problem identification phase, in prioritisation of causes of the problem during causal analysis phase, and in different stages of decision making. It uses the Pareto Principle (popularly known as the 80/20 rule) that 80% of the loss is due to 20% of the problems. Similarly, 20% of the causes are contributing to 80% of the problem.

Pareto analysis helps in separating the vital few problems from the trivial many.

The late quality guru, Joseph M Juran, came up with this principle in quality management and named it after Vilfredo Pareto, an Italian economist, who found that 20% of the population owned 80% of income in Italy, and some other countries.

The Pareto principle is applicable in many areas. Few examples:
- 20% of material in stores makes up 80% of inventory.
- 20% of SKUs make up 80% of warehouse stock of finished goods.

- 80% of customer complaints arise from 20% of company's products and services.
- 80% of customer complaints are because of 20% of defects.
- 80% of delays in schedule result from 20% of the possible causes for delays.

Pareto Diagram : Separates 'vital few' from 'trivial many'.
- Tool for prioritising problems.

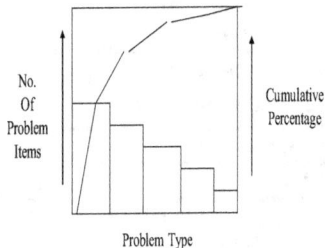

Exercise

Problem: Patient complaints in hospital are on the rise from 10 in a month to 845 in a month.

Target: To reduce patient complaints to zero.

Step 1: Data collection
Data on complaints by patients visiting hospital.
A check-list was prepared to record data for a month.

Category	Number of complaints
Incomplete Information provided	210
Appointments and schedules not adhered to	60
Cleanliness	92
Rude staff	13
Quality of treatment received	320
Too many formalities	75
Poor facilities	18
Waiting time	53
Others	4
	845

Step 2: Pareto analysis for prioritising- separating the vital few from the trivial many.

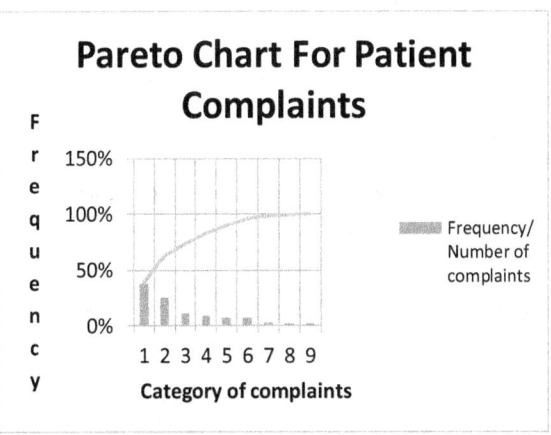

Legend for x axis
1.Quality of treatment received; 2. Incomplete information; 3. Cleanliness; 4. Too many formalities; 5. Appointments and schedules not adhered to; 6. Waiting time; 7. Poor facilities; 8. Rude staff; 9. Others

Focus areas- first set of priorities:

1. Quality of treatment received
2. Incomplete information
3. Cleanliness

12
Fish Bone Diagram

Fish bone diagram (or Ishikawa diagram named after Dr Kaoru Ishikawa, the Japanese quality guru) or cause and effect analysis, is a visual representation of the causes organised into major categories that contribute to a problem. The analysis is done when one is trying to find the possible causes of a problem and study the causal relationship. It can be made as a diagram, which is good for visual display, or in tabular form which is more convenient to prepare and list all possible causes. It identifies all possible causes and helps in tracing the root cause.

How to prepare a fish bone diagram?
1. Draw a solid centre line ending with a box at right hand side. The problem to be analysed is shown as the 'head' of the fish on the right-hand side box. This is the 'effect' part of cause and effect.
2. Draw slanting lines towards the central line being depicted as the 'bones' of the 'fish'. Label each bone of the fish. Use the typical six categories for labelling or

devise your own depending on the nature of the problem.
3. Write all possible causes on the branches off the cause category arrows.
4. Evaluate the possible causes and circle the most probable cause.

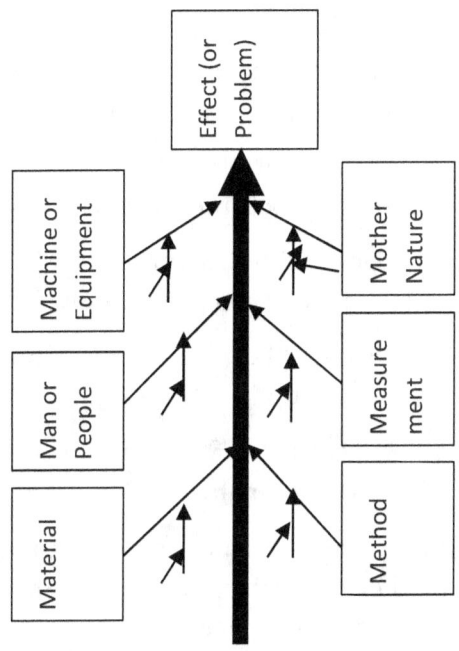

6Ms are the popular categories used for the classification of causes. However, these are not binding. One can group into different categories as per the problem. The broad, generalized 6M categories, are to trigger the thinking process and ensure that no probable cause is left out.

1. Man (or People): All those involved with the process

2. Method (or Process): Way of doing things, procedures, system.

3. Machine (or Equipment): Machines, equipment, computers, tools, etc.

4. Materials: Raw materials, components, consumables, stationery etc.

5. Measurement: for evaluation of quality, checking parameters.

6. Mother Nature (or Environment): Dust, storms, moisture, humidity, rains, temperature-low and high, location, time, and culture.

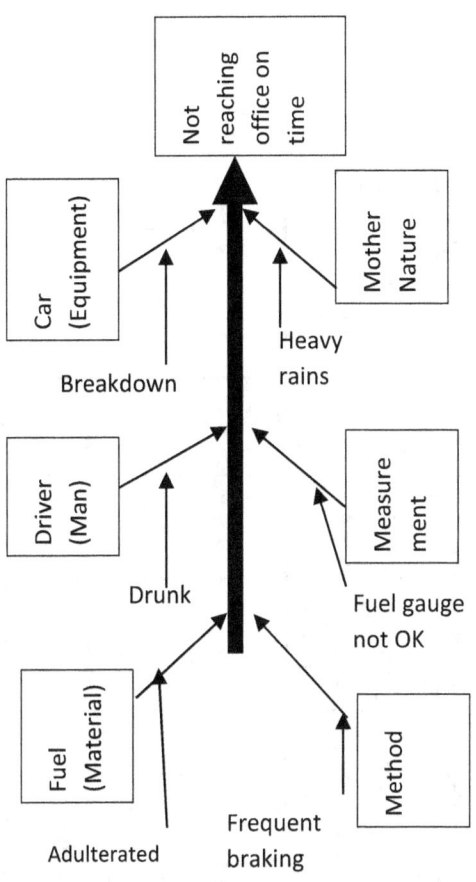

Fish Bone Diagram – Problem: Not reaching office on time

Cause and Effect - Tabular form

Effect or Problem

<Example> breakdowns of 100 hrs per month to be reduced to 10 hours/month

Main group	Primary cause 1st level	Secondary cause 2nd level	Tertiary cause 3rd level	Fourth level	Fifth level	Root cause	Countermeasure to remove the root cause	Action by Status
Man								
Material								
Method								
Machine								
Measurement								
Environment								

13
5W1H Analysis

5W1H is a questioning technique for critically examining a problem. First set of 5W1H questions helps in understanding the problem, the second set of questions facilitates in exploring alternatives, and the third set of 5W1H questions helps in identifying a solution to the problem.

This set of questions appeared in Rudyard Kipling's poem, and is also referred as the Kipling method:

"I keep six honest serving-men
(They taught me all I knew);
Their names are What and Why and When
And How and Where and Who."

Questions starting with What clarify the purpose, objective and need.

The When question relates to time, period, sequence.

The Who query is regarding the person who is doing the work.

Where relates to place, location, layout.

How question is about the method, process and system of doing work.

The Why question aims at understanding the reason behind each W and H.

5W 1H Analysis

The 5Ws

What	Where	When	Who
What is actually done? **Why?** What else might be done? What should be done? This tells the **Purpose** and helps in **Eliminating/Minimizing** unnecessary parts of the job.	**Where** is it being done? **Why?** Where else can we do? Where should we do? This tells the **Place** and helps in Location and Outsourcing Decisions.	**When** is it being done? **Why?** When else can we do? When should we do? This tells the **Sequence** and **Timing**, and gives ideas on changing timing, sequence.	**Who** is doing it? **Why?** Who else can do it? Who should do it? This tells the **Person** and helps in **Assigning jobs** training and development

H: How (Method, Process) is it being done? Why? How else? How should it be done? —Simplify, Combine, Improve the process

A modification is made by adding another W and H, and this is called 6W2H.

The additional W is Which, and H is how much.

For example, you are studying a machine breakdown problem where the root cause could be related to lubricant.

What is the process of lubrication? Why?
What other process can be used?
What should you use?

Which lubricant are you using? Why?
Which other lubricant can be used?
Which lubricant should we use?

How are you using the lubricant? Why that way?
How else can you apply?
How should you apply?

How much quantity is being used? Why?
How much should you use?
How do you measure the quantity? Why is measure required?
How else can you measure?
How should you measure?

Where is the lubricant being used? Why?

Where else can it be used?
Where should it be used?

When is the lubricant added? Why in that period?
When else?
When should you add lubrication?

Who does the adding of lubricant? Why that person?
Who else can do it?
Who should do?

The What question relates to Purpose and leads to eliminating or minimising unnecessary parts of the job. It helps in eliminating duplicacy or stopping a bad practice started years ago and which continues because nobody wants to break the precedent.

The Where question leads to investigation of the place, the location, the layout where work is happening. For example, Jack Welch must have asked in GE couple of decades before, 'where is our call centre,' and the answer would be U.S.A. 'Where else can we have call centres' would have resulted in answers like Philippines, Singapore, India, Honk Kong etc. Lastly, the question 'where we should have it,' and after detailed analysis and evaluation, the solution was Gurgaon, India.

The Who question is about the person. Whom do we assign the job? Who is doing the job currently? Is he a casual worker, a trained person or an overqualified person? Who else can do it? Finally, who should do it? These questions help in assigning the right person the right job and filling in training and development gaps in human resources.

When question is about time. When else and when should one do gives ideas about timing, sequencing, changing shift. For example, a steel company in Japan runs its operations at night and closes during the day because power charges are exorbitant during the day. In many companies, truck loading and unloading operations are carried during the day to reduce chances of theft and pilferage.

How relates to method. How else generates alternatives. There may be many process routes for making steel. The best alternative can be selected based on cost, productivity and quality performance. If the coke cost increases, the sponge iron route is economical, and if coke cost is low the blast furnace route is better.

Why must be asked at each stage so that the understanding of the problem and its causes is complete and not superficial.

14
Why.... Why Analysis

An integral part of Kaizen is Toyota's famous five-why analysis. Taiichi Ohno emphasised that true problem solving requires identifying 'root cause' as many times the root cause lies hidden beyond the source. The source of the problem may be a vendor or a machine as the problem occurs there. But finding the root cause requires one to dig deeper by asking why the problem occurred. The answer may lie in the purchase policy and not the vendor, or in poor planned maintenance management system and not the machine.

To appreciate the usefulness of Why..why questioning, observe how a child learns on his or her own. The child learns through continuous questioning till his parents get tired of answering. Initially, parents love their child asking questions and think the next Einstein is born in their family. Simple questions gradually become difficult for the parents as he or she asks why is the sky blue, from where did my baby sister come, why can't I carry mobile to class room, and so on. The father searches google at night and provides answers in the morning. The mother puts the onus of answering on the father, and the father pretends to be tired after work and avoids. In a scenario like this, the questioning of the child stops and so does his creativity. When the child goes to school, it is worse as the teacher does not listen and delivers lessons in a one-way communication mode. The child loses interest in learning and joins other friends in similar situation, moving away from a learning environment in an age most conducive to learning. When the same person goes to college, the lack of participation by teachers and students destroys the urge for learning. When he or she joins a job, within a few days they learn not to question the boss and always respond with a Yes Sir. Teaching or motivating people coming through such a learning journey is an extremely difficult task as one wants them to first unlearn, have an open and questioning mind, and the superiors have to support and encourage this thinking. Balancing disciplined systems approach in corporates with creative, lateral thinking, is tough.

<Example>

Why is the machine under breakdown?
Because the fuse has blown

Why has the fuse blown?
Because machine was running overloaded?

Why was the machine overloaded?
Because lubrication was not taking place

Why lubrication was missing?
Because oil pimp was not working?

Why was the oil pump not working?
Because the strainer was choked.

The root cause was choking of strainer. This was cleaned, the oil pump started working effectively, the lubrication was adequate, the machine was not overloaded, the fuse did not blow, and machine was running smoothly.

Frequency of cleaning of strainer should be decided and this should be put in the PM (Preventive Maintenance) schedule.

Ask "Why" Five times

Level of Problem	Corresponding level of countermeasure
There is a puddle of oil in the shop floor	Clean up the oil
Because the machine is leaking oil	Fix the machine
Because the gasket has deteriorated	Replace the gasket
Because we bought gaskets made of inferior material	Change gasket specifications
Because we got a good deal (price) on those gaskets	Change purchasing policies
Because the purchasing people get evaluated on short term cost savings	Change the evaluation policy for purchasing people

Why? Why? Why? Why? Why?

Source: The Toyota way by Jeffrey K Liker

15
FMEA Analysis

Failure Mode and Effect Analysis (FMEA) was adopted by the aerospace industry during 1960s. Today it has widespread use in the automotive industry. FMEA is a design and pre-product, process planning technique, which structures the thought process of managers and engineers to consider every conceivable way in which a product or component may fail.

FMEA enables engineers to look at all aspects of design and process in a formalised and structured way. The potential problems are recorded, numerically assessed and ranked in order, for action to be taken.

FMEA can be used for problems related to design improvements, process improvements, equipment performance improvement and function improvement.

It is an analytical technique which identifies potential failure modes, assesses potential effects to a customer, identifies potential causes of failure, identifies needs for changes, minimises potential cause of failure, facilitates inter departmental dialogue and facilitates identification of critical characteristics in a process.

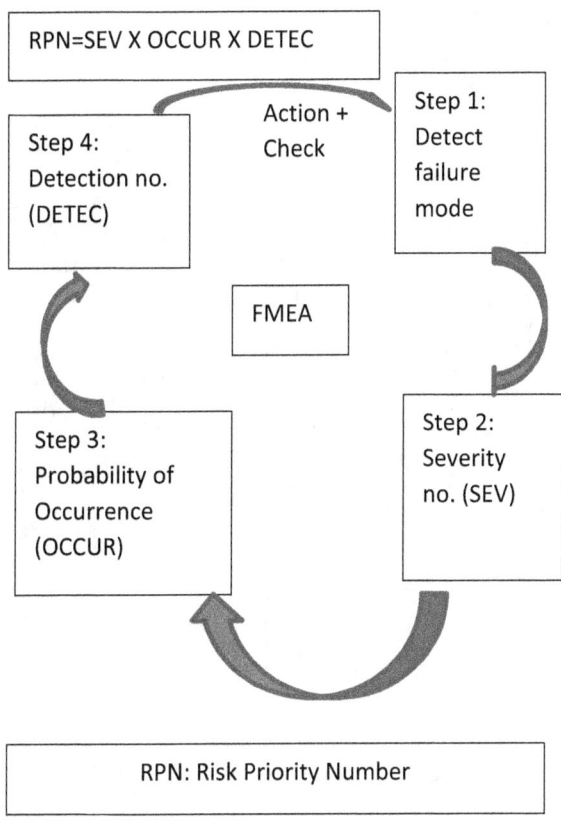

RPN: Risk Priority Number

Potential failure mode <Examples>

Bent, misaligned	Loose-wire, nut, handle	Open-wires, circuit
Corrosion, rust	Play, wear and tear	Uneven floor
Crack, scratch, dent	Leakages-air, water, gas etc.	Wrong material
Delayed delivery	Mix up of material	Wrong delivery-short or excess
Attrition	Stoppage	Accident
Data security breach	Customer complaints	Customer returns
Delayed payment	Contamination	Air pollution

FMEA Template

Rating is subjective in a scale of 1 to 10.

Process function requirement	Potential Failure Mode	Potential effects of failure	Severity	Potential Causes of failure	Probability of occurrence	Current Process Control	Detection	Risk Priority Number (RPN)	Recommended Action	Action taken	Action Taken and Results			
											New Severity	New Occurrence	New Detectability	New RPN

> Sample of a rating scale shown in next page.
> (Source: The Six Sigma Project Planner by Thomas Pyzdek).

Organisations make their scales as per their experience and requirements. As the 'before' and 'after' comparisons are with reference to the same scale, the measure of improvement will be correct.

Rating Scale ▼			
Rating	**Severity** How significant is the failure's effect to the customer	**Occurrence** How likely is the cause of this failure to occur	**Detectability** How likely is it that the existing system will detect the cause, if the defect occurs?
1	Minor: Customer won't notice the effect or consider it insignificant	Not likely	Nearly certain to detect before reaching the customer ($p=0$)
2	Customer will notice the effect	Documented low failure rate	Extremely low probability of reaching the customer without detection ($0<p<0.01$)
3	Customer will become irritated at reduced performance	Undocumented low failure rate	Low probability of reaching the customer without detection ($0.01<p<0.05$)
4	Marginal: Customer dissatisfaction due to reduced performance	Failures occur from time to time	Likely to be detected before reaching the customer ($0.05<p<0.20$)
5	Customer's productivity is reduced.	Documented moderate failure	Might be detected before reaching the customer ($0.20<p<0.50$)

Rating	Severity How significant is the failure's effect to the customer	Occurrence How likely is the cause of this failure to occur	Detectability How likely is it that the existing system will detect the cause, if the defect occurs?
6	Customer will complain. Repair or return likely.	Undocumented moderate failure rate	Unlikely to be detected before reaching the customer ($0.50 < p < 0.70$)
7	Critical. Reduced customer loyalty. Internal operations affected	Documented high failure rate	Highly unlikely to be detected before reaching the customer ($0.70 < p < 0.90$)
8	Complete loss of customer goodwill. Internal operations disrupted.	Undocumented high failure rate	Poor chance of detection ($0.90 < p < 0.95$)
9	Customer or employee safety compromised. Regulatory compliance failure	Failures common	Extremely poor chance of detection ($0.95 < p < 0.99$)
10	Catastrophic. Life risk without warning. Violation of law	Failures nearly always occur	Nearly certain that failure won't be detected ($p \sim 1$)
P=probability of failure not being detected			

<Exercise>

Prepare a FMEA chart for following problems:

1) Water supply from overhead tank:
   Failure modes could be non-availability of water, tank suddenly empty, overflowing water, low water level, motor damage, water meter running fast, bad quality water.
2) Guest lecture event on specific date and time:
   Failure modes could be guest speaker does not arrive, audio system does not work, stage collapses, multimedia presentation does not work, guest speaker is there but no audience, power fails, air conditioning fails, computer hangs, power point files does not open, flip chart is not there, background noise, illumination poor.
3) Baggage handling at Airport:
   Failure modes like belt stops, baggage mixed up, someone else takes away the baggage, baggage damaged, baggage handling excessive time, wrong display of flight number in baggage line.

16
Force Field Analysis

Force field analysis is a valuable change-management tool. It was developed by Kurt Lewin, an expert in experiential learning, group dynamics and action research.

In force field analysis, equilibrium is the status quo. Some of the forces are 'drivers' that move the system towards a desired goal. Other forces are 'restrainers' that prevent the desired movement and may even cause movement away from the goal. Team can design action plan to reduce restraints and increase drivers.

Making a Force field diagram:

1. Identify and understand the current state
2. Identify and understand the desired state
3. Identify and list driving forces acting to support the change.
4. Identify and list restraining forces acting to hinder the change.
5. For each force, designate the level of influence using a numerical scale e.g. 1=extremely weak and 7=extremely strong.

6. Chart the forces by listing the driving forces on the left and restraining forces on the right. Also chart the numbers allocated in step 5 next to their related force.
7. Evaluate the chart and determine whether change is viable.
8. Discuss how the change can be affected by decreasing the strength of the restraining forces or by increasing the strength of driving forces.
9. Discuss action strategies to eliminate the restraining forces and to capitalize on the driving forces.

Through conducting this process, a force field diagram is created.

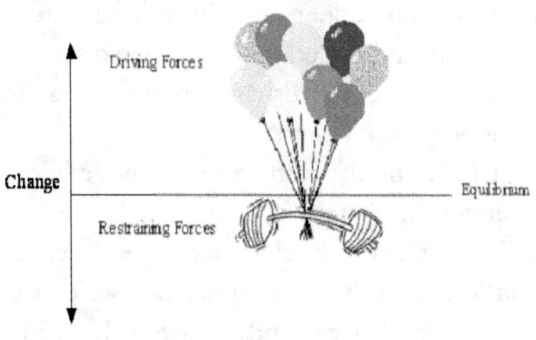

Helium filled balloons help in moving upwards, while the weights keep it down. The equilibrium is when the up thrust of helium gas matches the down thrust of weights.

Adding a balloon or removing a weight would cause a movement (change) upwards (positive).

Force Field Diagram-Invest in CNC m/c

Strength	Driving forces	Restraining forces	Strength
4	Increased productivity	Capital investment	5
3	Market opportunity	Inadequate marketing team	4
4	Increase in quality	Human interface	4
4	Cleanliness	Feudal mindset	3
5	Young manpower	Lack of training	3
20			19

⇐ No Change | Equilibrium | Change ⇒

Upgrade plant with new equipment

Strength	Driving forces	Restraining forces	Strength
5	Product range increase →	← Loss of overtime	3
6	High rate of output →	← Fear of new technology	5
5	Increase in quality →	← Higher cost	4
4	Reduce maintenance cost →	← Lack of capability	5
5	Less manpower →	← Loss of jobs	6
25			23

⟵ No Change | Equilibrium | Change ⟶

Buying a car

Strength	Driving forces	Restraining forces	Strength
6	Sale on now	High price	5
6	Attractive features	Want to invest in mutual funds	5
5	Low finance rate	Job insecure	6
4	Old car repair cost	Wife will want one car for herself	5
5	Status symbol	Children education	6
26			25

⬅ No Change | Equilibrium | Change ➡

17
Gantt Chart

Gantt chart is a graphic aid for project planning and control that displays the time line for each activity and is useful during implementation of the solution to the problem.

Steps to preparing a Gantt chart.
1. Create a three-column grid. Number and list all project activities in the left column. In the middle column, write the name of person/team/department responsible for the activity. The third column indicates the time frame and could be hours, days, weeks or months.
2. For each activity, draw a bar on the chart to indicate time frame for the activity.
3. Draw a triangle to indicate a major milestone.
4. The actual progress of the activity may be tracked vis a vis the plan in the same Gantt chart using different colour.
5. Software like MS Project can be used for preparing detailed and complex Gantt charts.

Activity	Responsible	Weeks						
		1	2	3	4	5	6	7
1.Brainstorm to identify problems	Kaizen team	▓						
2.Select problem	Kaizen team		▓					
3.Define problem	Kaizen team		▼					
4.Data collection	Anil, Akshay			▼				
5.Analyse problem	Kaizen team				▓			
6.Identify root cause	Kaizen team				▼			
7.Brainstorm and think out solution	Kaizen team					▓		
8.Implement solution	Suraj, Neeraj, Anil						▼	
9.Standardise and document	Akshay, Madhav						▓	
10.Monitor and Review	HOD							▼

18
Process Mapping

Process is an activity or a set of interdependent activities that will accomplish the desired goal. Using inputs provided by suppliers of these inputs, the process comprising of series of activities converts the input into the output desired by the individual or organisation's goal of meeting the expectations of the customer.

Process must add value. What does not add value is a Waste, and Waste is a problem which we need to resolve by eliminating or minimising Waste.

Process map is a management tool that visually describes the flow of work and enables us to understand the Value-added tasks and Non-value adding tasks or Waste. If the problem is described as a narration, understanding where, when and how waste is happening is difficult to grasp. Process mapping helps in this visualisation. Different mapping methods are used like Value Stream Mapping, Flow charts. Process flow chart, SIPOC diagram etc.

SIPOC diagram (Supplier, Input, Process, Output, Customer).

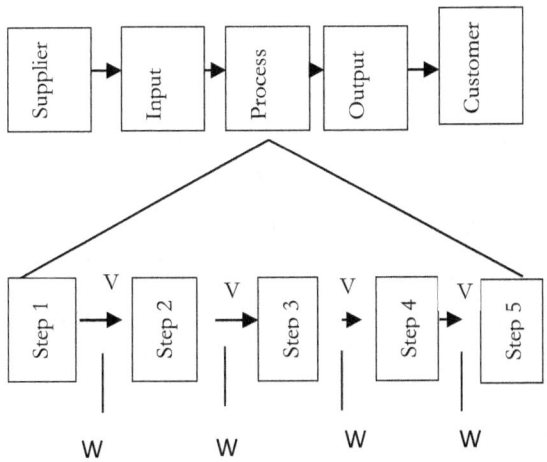

Value stream metrics: Time, Cost

V: Value add means contributing towards customer expectations

W: Wasteful practices, products and services that do not add Value. For example, delays, excess storage, scrap generated, defects, rework, idling, breakdowns, slow speed, excess movement and transportation, incorrect process.

Value based process maps

- What adds Value here?

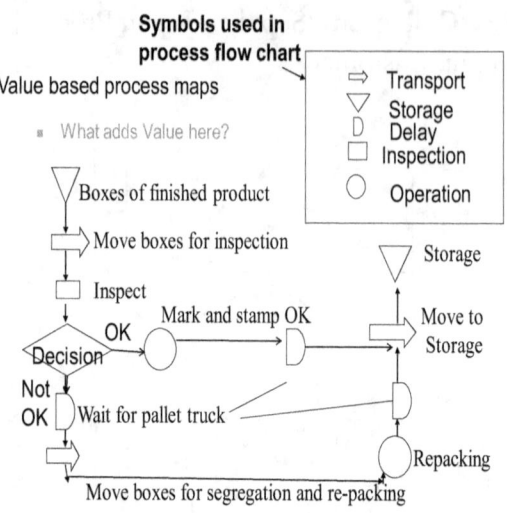

Symbols used in process flow chart

⇒ Transport
▽ Storage
D Delay
□ Inspection
○ Operation

<Exercise>

- ## Analysis of Operation of Going to Work
  - John is always late for office. The office starts at 9 a.m and John's attendance record for last three months is as under:

	Late within 15 mins	Late 15-24 mins	Late 25 to 30 mins
June	2 times	8 times	10 times
July	5 times	9 times	12 times
Aug	3 times	12 times	11 times

Problem.

John is late in reaching office. He must improve. John must reach office 10 minutes before the scheduled start at 9a.m on all occasions (100% of the time).

Can you help John in making a process chart for analysing his problem?

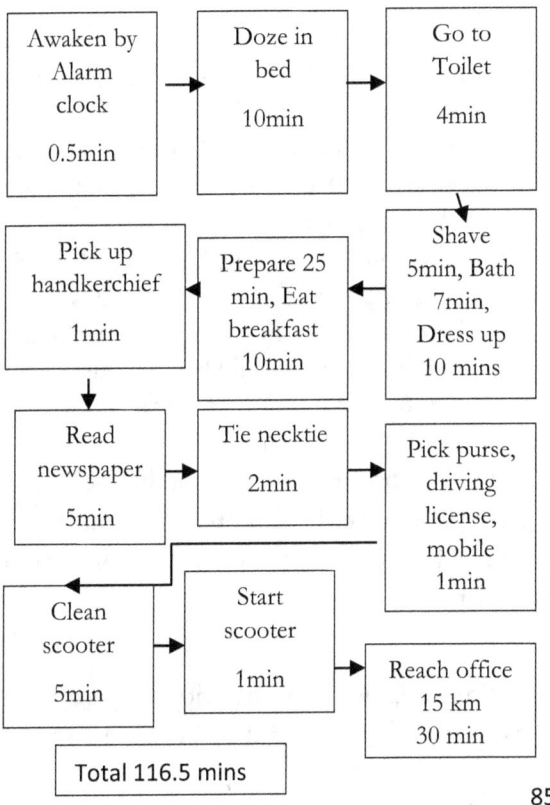

19
Control Charts

Control charts assist in tracking the process variation and distinguishing between assignable causes and chance causes of variation.

Process variations are traceable to two kinds of causes:

- Chance (or random) causes which are inherent in the process. This variation is because of the chosen technology, process, equipment. For example, variation in blood pressure, pulse rate of a normal, healthy person.
- Assignable (or special) causes which cause excessive variation. For example, belt loose, alignment not proper, play, person not skilled, dust in environment, high temperature.

Ideally only chance causes should be present in a process because these represent a stable and predictable process which leads to minimum variation.

A process that is operating without assignable causes of variation is said to be "in a state of statistical control." The control chart for such a process has all the data points within the statistical control limits.

The objective of a control chart is not to achieve a state of statistical control as an end but to reduce variation.

The control chart distinguishes between chance and assignable causes through its choice of control limits. These are calculated using laws of probability in such a way that highly improbable causes of variation are presumed to be due not to random or chance causes but to assignable or special causes.

When the variation exceeds the statistical control limits, it is a signal that assignable causes have entered the process and the process should be investigated to identify these causes of variation.

Random variation within the control limits means that only random causes are present; the amount of variation has stabilised, and minor process adjustments should be avoided.

Note that a control chart detects the presence of an assignable cause but does not find the cause-that task must be handled by a subsequent investigation of the process.

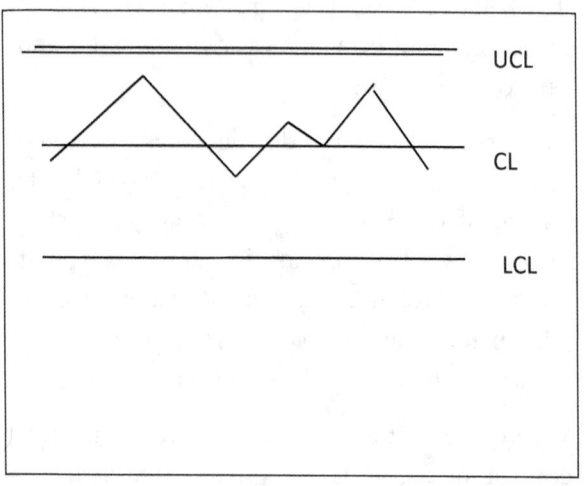

UCL Upper Control Limit

CL   Central Limit

LCL Lower Control Limit

Please note these are not specification limits. Control limits are based on sigma of the process and are placed at plus 3 sigma and minus 3 sigma respectively. Central limit is the mean value.

If data points lie between the control limits and are not showing a run trend in any one direction, the process is stable and only random (chance) causes are the reason for variation. In such cases, there is no need to disturb the process.

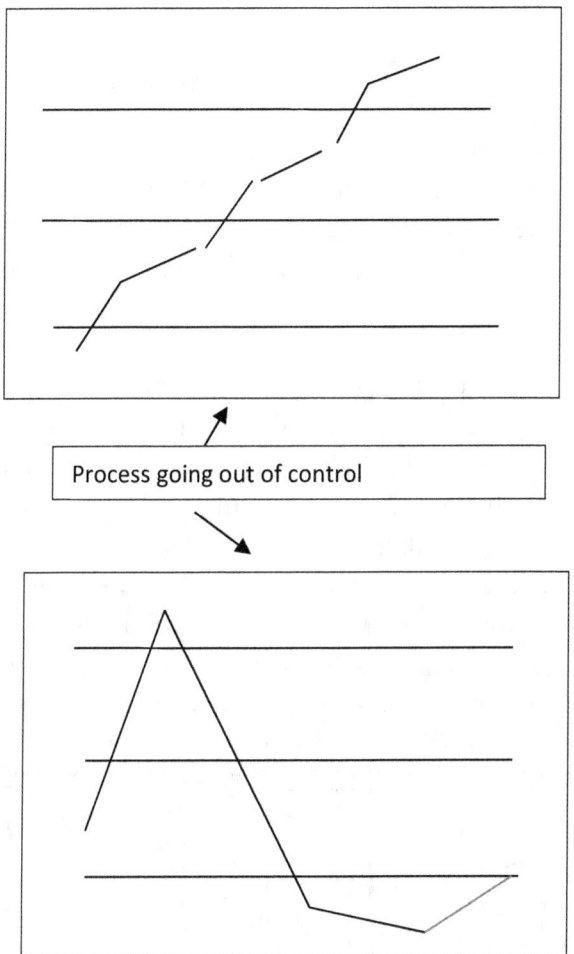

20
Affinity Diagram

This tool is effective for cutting through the confusion and bringing problem clearly into view when the nature of the problem is not clear, data is verbal and qualitative, and the team is confused.

The topic is selected, and brainstorming done to collect verbal data. The data is supplemented with observation, opinions and interviews. Each item of verbal information is written on a data card. After the data cards have been prepared, one spots cards that seem most nearly related, that is, have an affinity for each other. The statements on similar cards are combined into a single statement and this new card is called the affinity card.

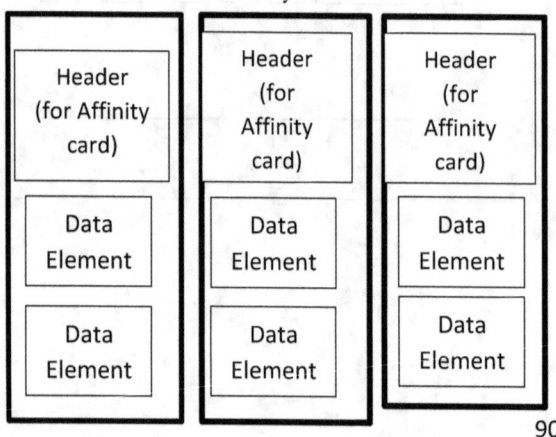

<Example> When brainstorming, one can write on post it stickers, put the stickers on a board/chart paper, and later flip them around to put them under appropriate headers.

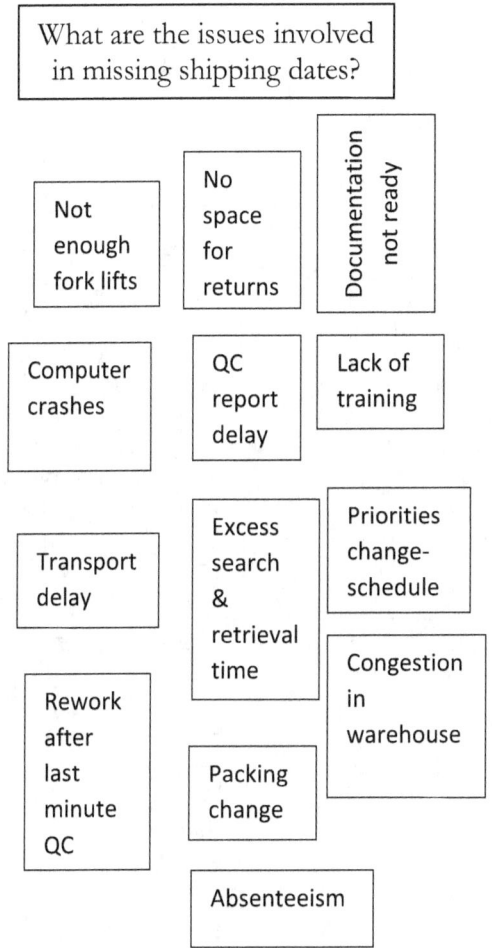

Affinity diagram for above example

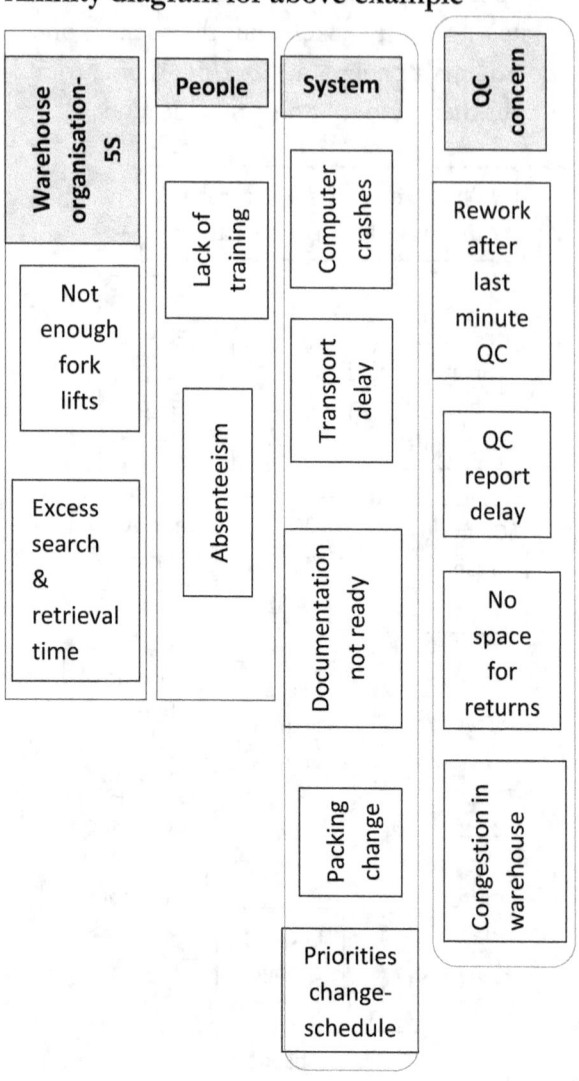

21
Interrelationship (Relations)Diagram

Interrelationship diagram is a tool for resolving complex issues by unravelling the logical connections between intertwined causes and effects. It develops a person's thinking and helps in picking out the important factors from an amorphous mass of cause and effects.

Express the problem in a form that indicates that the desired outcome is not being achieved; for example, "Why isn't X happening?" Write this in red on a card or post it sticker. Let each member of the group think of five causes affecting the problem and write these in black on separate cause cards. Group similar cards together. By repeatedly asking Why, systematically explore the cause and effect relationships and place the causes most closely related to the problem nearest to the problem card. Connect all cards by arrows showing cause and effect relationships.

Look for relationships among group of causes. Connect related groups with arrows. For selecting most important causes, use a scoring system (for example, each team member assigns 2 points to a very important cause and 1 point to a less important one). Analyze the diagram- Count the arrows (# out - # in). Highest out are primary drivers.

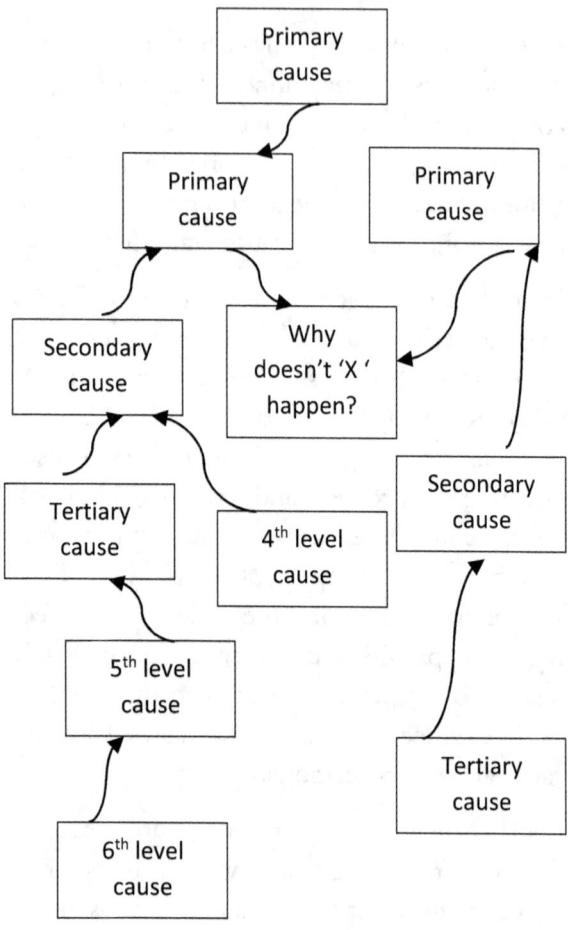

<Example> What are the issues related to reducing litter?

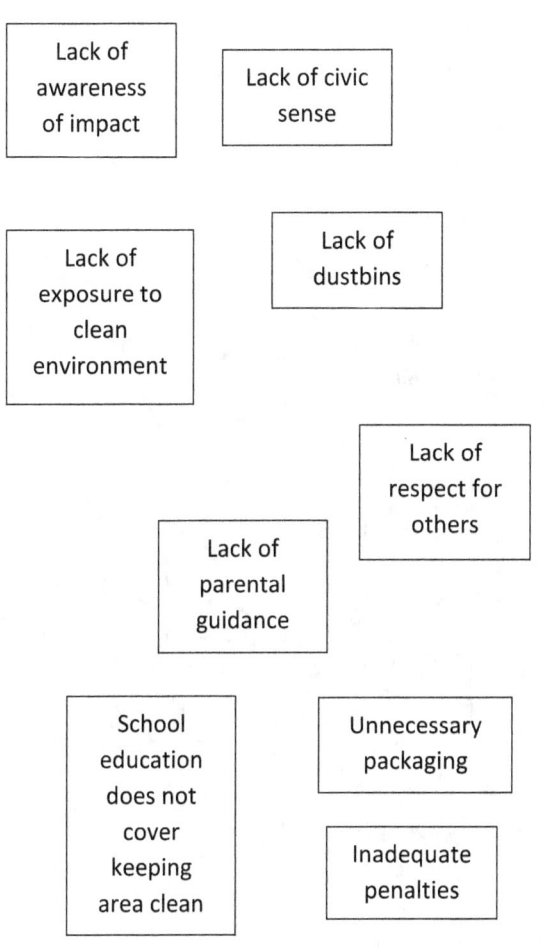

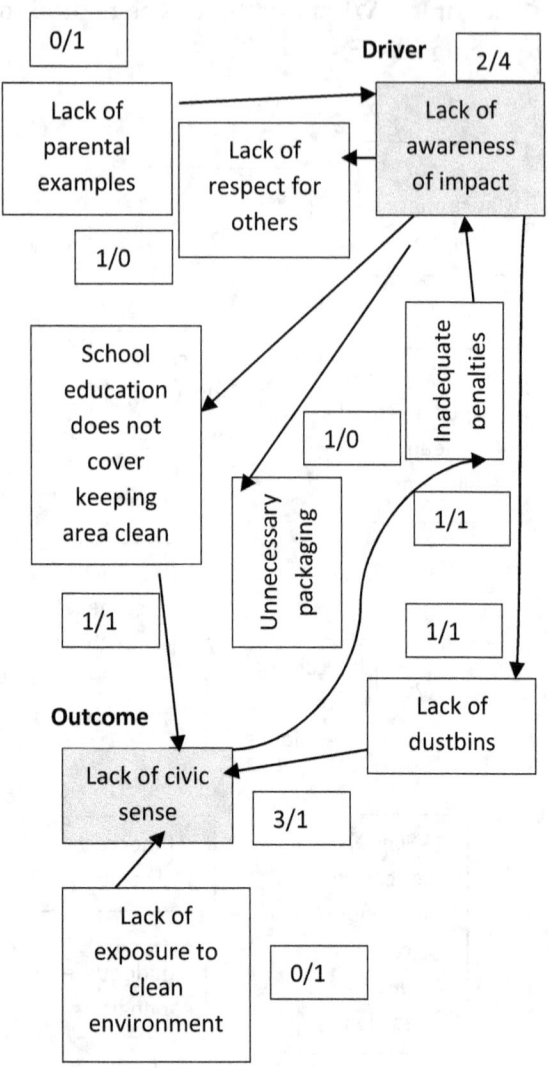

22
Tree Diagram

Once a relations diagram has been used to identify causes of a problem, next step is to find a way of eliminating those causes. Constructing Tree diagram facilitates analysis through systematic and logical enumeration of the causes.

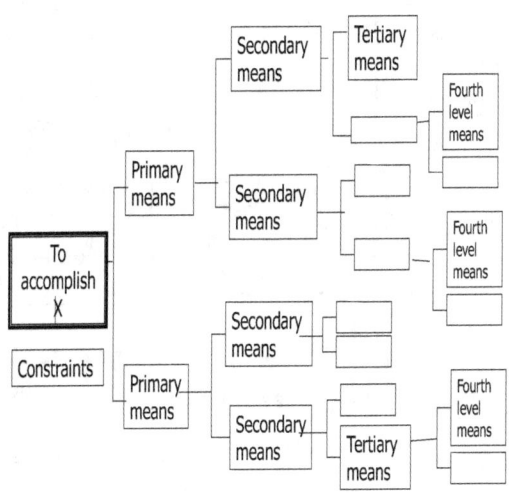

<Example>

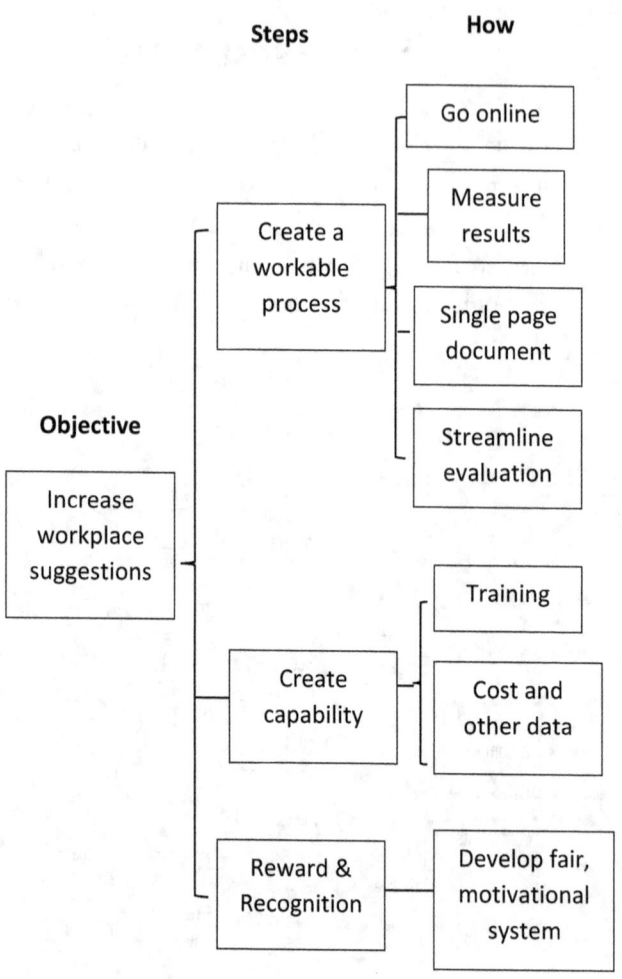

23
Matrix diagram

Matrix diagrams can be used for evaluating the strategies developed by means of a tree diagram and allocating responsibility for implementing them. For example, they can be used for quality deployment for investigating the correspondence between a set of customer product requirements and a related set of design quality characteristics. Similarly design quality requirements with process quality requirements and process quality requirements with process control requirements.

The matrix diagram below organizes data into sets of items to be compared. It shows relationships and/or evaluates the strengths of relationships between the items in each set.

Use of few problem-solving tools			
	Creativity	Analysis	Action
Brainstorming	□		
Fish bone	®	□	▲
Pareto		□	
Affinity chart	□	□	▲
Gantt chart		®	□

Legend: □ Always, ® Frequently, ▲ Occasionally

<Example>

Item 1 and Item A are strongly related.

Technical requirements → / Customer requirements ↓	Item A	Item B	Item C	Item D	Item E	Total relationship strength
Item 1	®	▲			○	13
Item 2			®	○		12
Item 3		▲			▲	2
Item 4	○		▲	®		13
Item 5				○		
	12	2	10	15	4	

Symbol	Relationship	Value
®	Strong	9
○	Medium	3
▲	Weak	1

The scoring can be used for prioritising and taking decisions on which items and attributes to focus on and invest in better design and material. Technical requirements shown as Item E and Item B have weak relationship with customer requirements shown as item 1 and 3.

24
Arrow Diagram

The tree diagram or a matrix diagram helps in deciding the best possible strategies for solving a problem. Arrow diagrams are for Action Planning - when and in what order the implementation must be carried out. The arrow diagram shows the required order of tasks in a project or process, the best schedule for the entire project, and potential scheduling and resource problems and their solutions. The arrow diagram lets one calculate the "critical path" of the project.

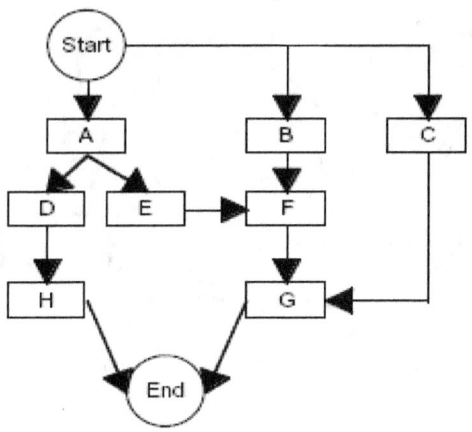

Node	Activity	Time (weeks)	Precedence
0	Get land	12	Nil
1	Construct building	24	1
2	Place order for equipments	8	1
3	Install equipments	20	1,2
4	Function test	4	3
5	Recruit	12	0
6	Train	4	5
7	Trial run	2	4,6
8	Commercial run	1	7

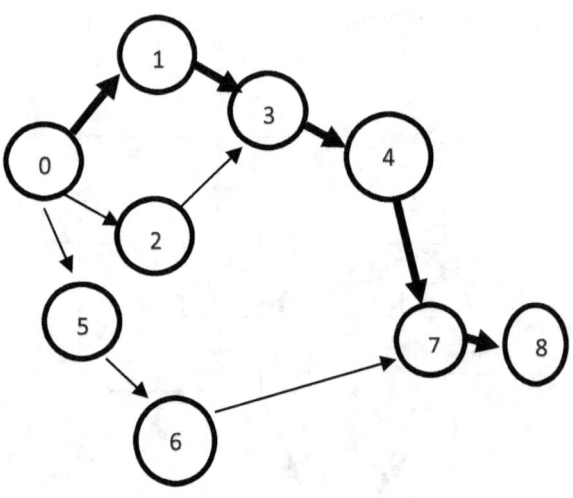

Critical path ➡ 0>1>3>4>7>8 = 63 weeks

25
Process Decision Program Chart

Process Decision Program Charts (PDPCs) are used for planning activities when information is incomplete, situation fluid and difficult to forecast. The goal is to depict events and contingencies likely to occur when progressing from a starting point to one or more final outcomes. PDPC consists of series of steps linked in sequence by arrows. For example – planning an R&D project, mapping out countermeasures against long term chronic problems, planning sales campaign.

PDPC maps out all contingencies when moving from statement of purpose to its realization. It is another form of tree diagram where the objective is contingency planning. In first level, the purpose is defined. Then in second level, the activities are stated, while the third level gives the steps to be taken in these activities. The fourth level puts the what if questions (continencies) and the fifth level gives the countermeasure as answer to each what if.

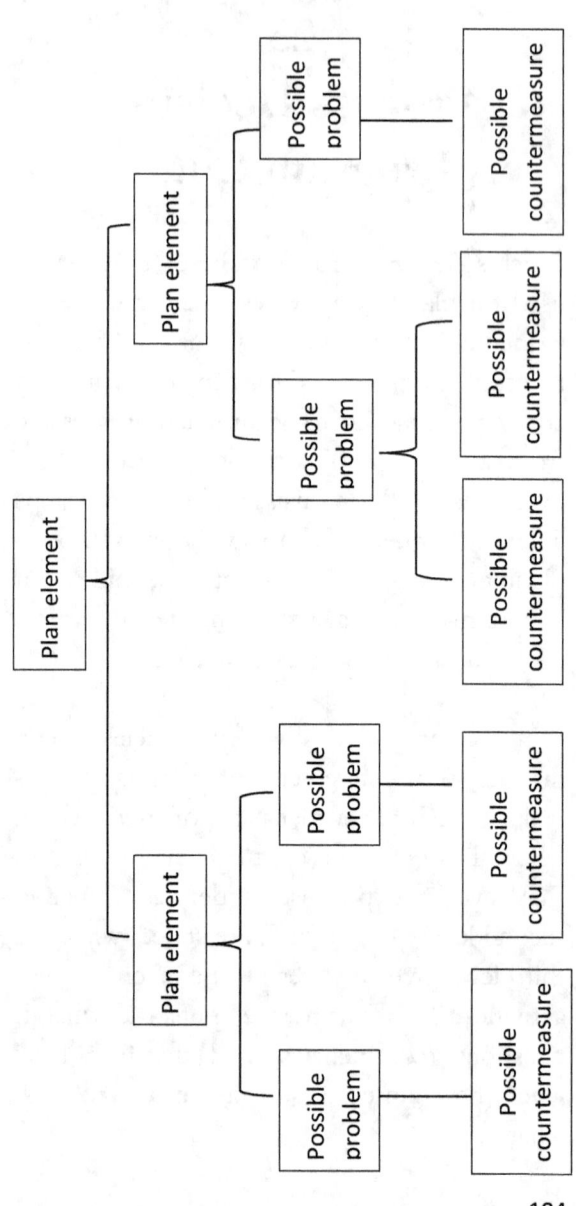

\<Example\>

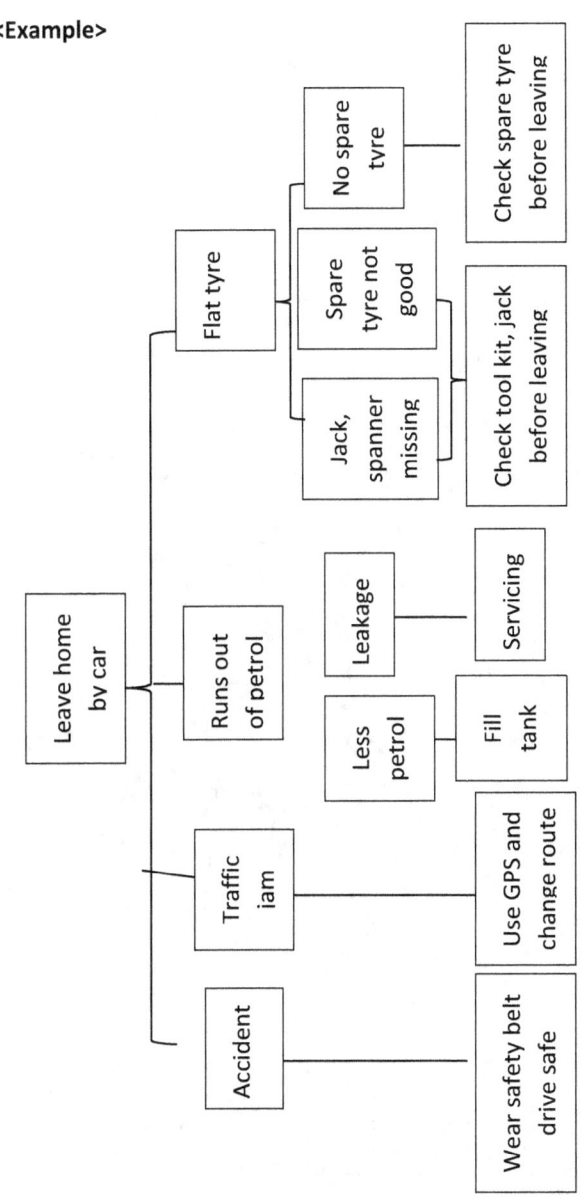

26
Mind Mapping

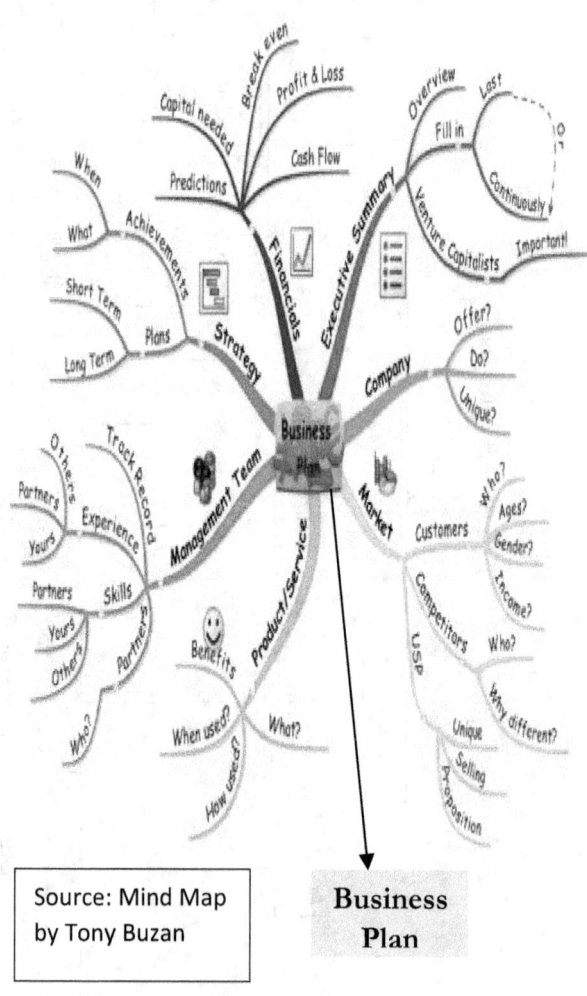

Source: Mind Map by Tony Buzan

Business Plan

A mind map is a diagram, created around a single concept, to visually organise information in hierarchical way showing relationship among pieces of the whole.

The term 'mind map' was popularised by Tony Buzan, and is useful in brainstorming, learning, visual thinking and problem solving. It is a tool that captures the thinking that goes on inside one's brain and makes a person a better thinker and creator of ideas.

Mind map is made by starting in the centre with an image of the topic. Images, symbols, codes, colours and key words are used. Each word/image is connected starting from the central word/image. The lines become thinner as they radiate out from the centre. It allows the mind to wander.

Mind maps make use of word associations, encouraging one to follow one's own thought patterns. As opposed to traditional note taking as a linear text, mind mapping is both analytical and artistic and engages the brain in a richer way helping in all its cognitive functions.

Making mind maps is fun. In one single chart, it displays all ideas and points related to the theme. For example, the mind map shown above visualises the making of a business plan needed by entrepreneurs and investors.

27
Benchmarking

Benchmarking is the process of continually searching for the best methods, practices and processes, and either adopting or adapting their good features and implementing them to become the "best of the best."

Benchmarking helps in identifying gaps, otherwise how does one know whether the work one is doing is the best, average or poor. The gap is the current level of performance, called the 'baseline,' and the desired level of performance based on a benchmark.

The benchmark may be from neighbourhood, what is best within the organisation which is termed as the internal benchmark. Like you may benchmark with the best boy or girl in your class in co-curricular activities. After the internal benchmark is reached, you may benchmark best practices and performance in competing organisations, or with any similar process. Finally, the benchmark should be with world class organisations.

Like it happens with Olympic records, benchmarks are meant to be broken and new benchmarks created.

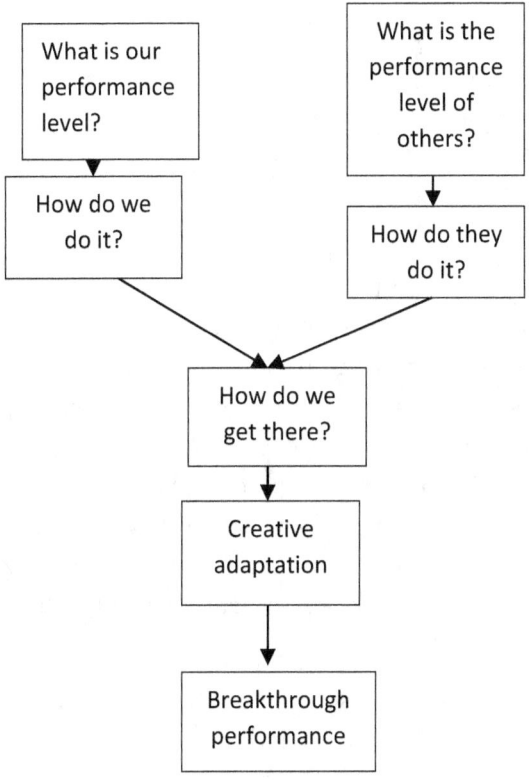

Benchmark	Level
Best in world	7
Best in country	6
Best in process	5
Leader-industry, school, any organisation	4
Best in region	3
Internal-best in company, school etc	2
Baseline-current level	1

Benchmarking can be used at the stage of problem identification. Sometimes we get stuck with no problems in our basket. If it were true, it is excellent, but unfortunately problems exist all around us, and only discovery of problems leads to progress. When stuck, ask yourself how others are doing. How are other nations doing? How are other societies performing? How competitors are faring? How and why another department or an individual is doing better?

There is a Hindi song 'I am the best..' played by Shahrukh Khan and sung by Abhijeet. Proclaiming I am the best is good for self-publicity and marketing, but if one really thinks that he is the best, then he has closed all doors for identifying and solving problems.

28
Data Analysis-few more tools

Testing of hypothesis

Hypothesis testing is a statistical decision – making process in which inferences are made about the population from a sample. It begins with an assumption called a hypothesis that we make about a population parameter. Then we collect sample data and use sample statistics to decide if the hypothesis is true. Suppose the unit head of a plant says the OEE (overall equipment effectiveness) is 90% in his plant. The sample statistic reveals OEE of 88% and standard deviation of 1.02%. Should we accept the unit head's hypothesis?

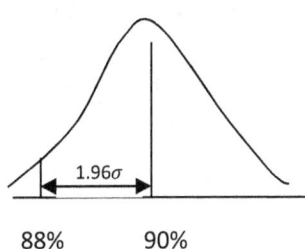

88%   90%

The null hypothesis is that population mean OEE is 90%.

$H_o : \mu = 90\%$

The probability of OEE going below 88% is 2.5%. If the level of significance is more than 2.5%, we will accept the hypothesis.

Because of sampling, hypotheses testing is subject to error. A Type I error occurs if the null hypothesis is rejected when it is true. Conversely, a Type II error occurs if the null hypothesis is accepted when it is false.

<Example>

A manufacturing unit of lawn mowers has committed to its client that the life of the lawn mower is 250 hours before it starts experiencing problems and needs service. The data of field tests on 10 lawn mowers shows that they required service after 205, 430, 301, 199, 222, 124, 89, 289, 260 and 214 hours. Based on this data, can the manufacturer make this claim to its client, at a significance level of 0.05?

205, 430, 301, 199, 222, 124, 89, 289, 260 and 214

	205
	430
	301
	199
	222
	124
	89
	289
	260
	214
mean=	233.3
std dev=	95.64756
σ_x	30.24641
t=	-0.1746

at alpha=0.05 (one tail), and 9d.f, t=1.833
hence accept the hypothesis that lawn mowers have life greater than 250 hr

Steps:

1. Use hypothesis testing to determine from analysis of a sample that the entire population possesses a certain property.
2. Decide whether this is a two tailed or one tailed test. State the hypothesis. Select a level of significance appropriate to this decision.
3. Decide which distribution (t or z) is appropriate and find the critical value for the chosen level of significance.
4. If the sample statistic is within the acceptance region, accept H_0. Else reject H_0.

5. Translate the statistical results into appropriate managerial action.

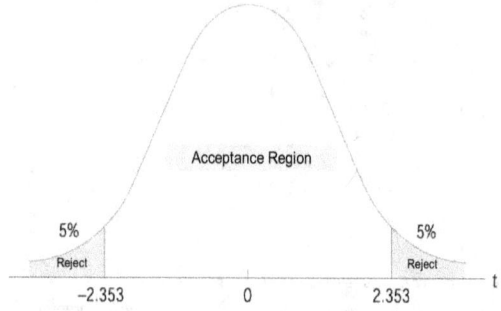

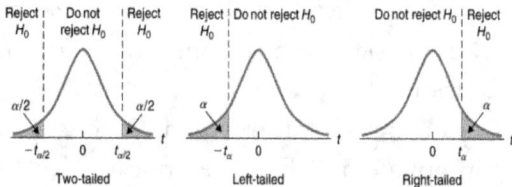

ANOVA (Analysis of Variance)

ANOVA enables testing for the significance of the differences among more than two sample means. Using analysis of variance, one will be able to make inferences about whether the samples are drawn from population having the same mean. For example, testing which of the five training methods provide the fastest learning, comparing the mileage achieved by four different brands of petrol, effect on yield by varying parameters like temperature, pressure and addition of catalyst.

Steps:
1. To determine if several samples come from populations with equal means, use ANOVA.
2. For inferences about the variance of one population, use the chi-square distribution with n-1 degrees of freedom.
3. For inferences about the variances of two populations, use the F distribution with n_1-1 and n_2-1 df.
4. Determine between column variance, within column variance and their ratio F.
5. If the sample statistic falls within the acceptance region, accept H_0. Else reject H_0.

6. Translate the statistical results into appropriate managerial action.

One can use Excel for doing ANOVA by adding Analysis Tool Pak.

Regression

In regression analysis, using historical data, one develops an estimating equation, a mathematical formula, that relates the known variables to the unknown variable. After knowing the pattern of the relationship, one can apply correlation analysis to determine the degree to which the variables are related. The known variable is the independent variable, and the variable, one is trying to predict, is the dependent variable.

Simple (Linear or curvilinear) regression makes use of one independent variable. To improve the accuracy of the estimate, one can add more independent variables and the process is called multiple regression.

Computer software like SPSS, Minitab, SAS, MYSTAT can be used for estimating the multiple or simple regression equation and forecasting the value of dependent variable.

Simple regression
$y = a + bx$

Multiple regression
$y = a + b_1x_1 + b_2x_2 + b_3x_3 + b_4x_4 + \ldots + b_ix_i$
where x_i is the independent variable and y the dependent variable, like sales can be the dependent variable, and factors like advertisement, promotion, pricing, inflation, bank interest etc can be the independent variables.

Design of experiments (DOE)

In many improvement projects, the true causes of the problem jump out when a team uses simple methods like creating process maps and charting data. But in other situations, it's not clear what caused the problem. Or there are many process parameters to consider that it appears nearly impossible to find the right combination to provide optimal performance.

The tool of choice under these situations is DOE. It is a method used for testing and optimizing the performance of a process, product, service, or solution. It uses tests of statistical significance, correlation and regression to learn about the behaviour of a product or service under varying conditions. It provides opportunity to plan and control the variables using an experiment, as opposed to just gathering and observing real-world events in the manner known as "empirical observation".

Basic Steps in DOE
① Identify the factors to be evaluated.
What do you want to learn from the experiment? What are the likely influences on the process or product? Balance the benefit of getting additional data by testing more factors with the increased cost and complexity.
② Define the "levels" of the factors to be tested. The variable factors are like speed, time, temperature, pressure, weight etc.
③ Create an array of experimental combinations. In DOE, one wants to avoid the "one factor at a time" approach, where each variable is tested in isolation. Arrays of conditions are examined to get representative data for all the factors
④ Conduct the experiment under the prescribed conditions.
⑤ Evaluate the results and conclusions. Tools like ANOVA and Multiple Regression are used.

Improve

29
Six Thinking Hats

Finding solutions to problems requires creative thinking. One way to sharpen the thinking skills and to generate innovative solutions is to use the concept of six thinking hats. Dr Edward de Bono pioneered the concept of creative thinking using six thinking hats. This is best experienced in group working. It helps expand thinking and gain new insights by looking at a problem from different perspectives.

Each thinking hat is a different style of thinking. There is no particular order in which the thinking hats must be used. One can start with the blue hat followed by the green hat, white hat and yellow hat. The black hat will question and give counterpoints to the yellow and the green hat. Red hat can enter at any stage.

The six thinking hats are explained below:
① **White hat**- concerned with data and information available and needed. The facts, just the facts.

② **Red hat**- concerned with feelings, hunches, likes, dislikes, fears, emotions and intuition.
③ **Black hat**- judgment, the "devil's advocate," points out the weakness in our thinking, cautions against acceptance of idea without questioning it. Discussing why the solution to the problem will not work, its existing and potential downsides, and brainstorming where things can go wrong, is the job of the black hat.
④ **Yellow hat**- symbolises brightness, optimism and represents logical, positive aspects of thinking. It explores positives and looks for benefits and value.
⑤ **Green hat**- "creativity hat" is for alternatives, creative ideas and possibilities, new concepts, new perceptions, and does not need to have logical base
⑥ **Blue hat**- is for "process control." It manages the thinking process itself.

White hat questions:
What information is available? What can we learn from it? Look for gaps. What information would we like to have? What information do we need? How are we going to get the missing information? This could be by analyzing past trends and extrapolating historical data.

Red hat questions:
What are my feelings right now? What does my intuition tell me? What is my gut reaction?

The red hat should be limited to 30 seconds or less. It gives full permission to express feelings, hunches and intuitions, and does not require one to justify or explain the reasons for one's feelings. It can be used as part of thinking that leads to decision. It can also be used after a decision is made.

Black hat questions:
What could be the possible problems? What can some of the difficulties be? What are points of caution? What are the risks?

The black hat explores why something may not work. It looks at things cautiously, pessimistically and defensively. It must have logical reasons for concerns.

Black hat is a powerful assessment tool when used after the yellow hat. It highlights the weak points in a plan and forces one to think contingency measures to counter problems that may arise. It supplies a road map for improvement and problem solving when used before and after the green hat. One should not overuse the black hat.

Yellow hat questions:
What are the benefits? What are the positives? Is there a concept in the idea that looks attractive? Can this be made to work?

The yellow hat requires a deliberate effort. It reinforces creative ideas and new directions. It must give reasons why the idea is valuable or might work. It complements the black hat.

Green hat questions:
Are there other ways to do this? What else could we do here? What are the possibilities? What will overcome our difficulties?

The green hat encourages search for new ideas and alternatives and sets up a micro culture for creativity, allowing for suggestions without having to support them logically. It balances the natural dominance of the black hat.

Blue hat questions:
What is our agenda? What is our next step? What hat are we using now? How can we

summarise the discussion so far? What is our decision?

The blue hat is usually the role of the facilitator and focuses and refocuses thinking.

Summary	
White Hat	Facts and Information
Red Hat	Feelings and Intuition
Yellow Hat	Benefits and positivity
Black Hat	"Devil's Advocate"- caution, 'what can go wrong' concerns.
Green Hat	Creativity-generating creative ideas, innovative solutions, alternatives
Blue Hat	Process control, organising thinking process, logical

30
Poka Yoke

Japanese Guru Shingeo Shingo propounded the concept of 'Zero Quality Control-ZQC' using poka yoke devices. Poka Yoke are creative devices that make it nearly impossible for an operator to make an error, or 'defects=zero.' The initial term was baka-yoke, which means 'fool-proofing.' In 1963, a worker at Arakawa Body Company refused to use baka-yoke mechanisms in her work area, because of the term's dishonorable and offensive connotation. Hence, the term was changed to poka-yoke, which means 'mistake-proofing.' Japanese word Poka Yoke derived from *yokeru* (to avoid) and *poka* (inadvertent errors).

Poka-yoke (pronounced POH-kah YOH-kay) devices are used either to prevent the special causes that result in defects, or to inexpensively inspect each item that is produced to determine whether it is acceptable or defective.

A poka-yoke device is any mechanism that either prevents a mistake from being made or makes the mistake obvious at a glance. The ability to find mistakes at a glance is essential because, as Shingo says, "The causes of defects lie in worker errors, and defects are the results of neglecting those errors. It follows that mistakes will not turn into defects if worker errors are discovered and eliminated beforehand." "Defects arise because errors are made; the two have a cause-and-effect relationship. ... Yet errors will not turn into defects if feedback and action take place at the error stage."

Shingo's example: A worker is assembling a device that has two push-buttons. A spring must be put under each button. Error: Sometimes a worker forgets to put the spring under the button and a defect occurs. Poka Yoke: The worker counts out two springs from a bin and places them in a small dish. After assembly is complete, if a spring remains in the dish, an error has occurred. The operator knows a spring has been omitted and can correct the omission immediately. The cost of this inspection (looking at the dish) is minimal, yet it effectively functions as a form of inspection.

A defect is a product that deviates from specification or does not meet customer expectations. An error is any deviation from the intended process. All defects are created by errors which could be as follows:

- Missing steps in standard operating procedures (SOPs)
- Missing parts
- Mix up
- Wrong item
- Process omissions, missing steps, skipping specifications of product
- Machine error, set up error, tooling error
- Utility conditions-water, electricity, air, gas etc. -not within quality standards
- Human errors

Poka Yoke way of problem solving thinks through the causes of errors and designs a way of stopping the errors before a problem occurs. The product should be designed such that it cannot be assembled incorrectly.

Strict discipline in following three simple rules can minimize problems:

1. Do not accept faulty item from previous process (wear the cap of a customer).
2. Do not make a faulty item (wear the cap of a quality producer).
3. Do not pass on a faulty item to the next process (wear the cap of a quality supplier).

The causes of human errors are to be considered while designing Poka Yoke. The common causes are:

- Forgetfulness
- Wrong identification
- Misunderstanding
- Lack of standardisation
- Willful (ignoring rules or procedure)
- Lack of experience, training
- Inadvertent, sloppy
- Tired, sleepy
- Intentional (Sabotage)

Approaches to Poka-Yoke:

1. Prevention – steps taken so that error does not happen.

2. Control – steps to remove defective items or shut down process if errors are being made.

3. Detection – warning signals to stop the process and correct the problem through beeps, lights, alarms or automatic shutdown of system.

Color coding is also an effective non-automatic option.

Poka-yoke systems consist of three primary methods:

1. Contact (for example limit switch), non-contact (for example proximity switches, photo electric switch). For example, in hotel rooms the insertion of key on keycard power switch automatically switches on power and switches off when the key is taken out when the guest leaves the room. Stove burner switches off when pot or pan is removed. Airplane lavatory lights come on only when the door lock is engaged. This keeps customers from failing to lock the door.

2. Counting type- for example sensor that counts the number of times a part is used, or a process is completed and releases the part only when the right count is reached. For example, packing 50 items in a box- the packing will not start till 50 items have been loaded.

3. Sequencing – ensures steps are performed in right order to get the desired performance. The idea is to use sensors to determine if a motion or a step in a process has occurred. If the step has not occurred or has occurred out of sequence, then the

sensor signals a timer or other device to stop the machine and signal the operator. For example, in cement bagging operation, the conveyor will not move to the stitching process till the weighment of bags is complete. For safety, lifts are designed not to start till the door is closed. Similarly, in various online bookings and form filling processes, like the visa application process, the next sequence steps (the next page) cannot be initiated till the previous steps (filling all the data fields of previous page) have been completed.

The USB connector cannot be connected in the wrong way because of its inner shape.

Different shapes for each connector prevent wrong usage.

You can see many applications of Poka Yoke around you. Circuit breakers prevent electrical overloads and the fires that result. Certain toothbrushes have colored bristles that become clear at the tips of the bristles through use. Similarly, in razor blades (Gillette make) the green color fades to white with usage. The colour coding of wires and cables assists in identification. The torque driver ensures that all bolts are tightened to the desired torque-not less, not more. Water level sensor switch ensures the pump is switched off when the tank is full.

If a tightening process is performed a fixed number of times, say on six bolts, a simple poka-yoke device would incorporate the use of a wrench dipped in diluted paint. Since untightened bolts will not have paint on them, the operator can easily see if he or she has performed the process the required number of times.

31
Lateral Thinking

Lateral thinking is a term coined by Edward de Bono, psychologist, physician and writer. It first appeared in the title of his book *The Use of Lateral Thinking*, published in 1967. De Bono defines lateral thinking as methods of thinking concerned with changing concepts and perception.

Lateral thinking, or 'out of the box' thinking as popularly expressed, is about reasoning that is not immediately obvious and about ideas that may not be obtainable by using only traditional step-by-step logic. Techniques that apply lateral thinking to problems are characterized by the shifting of thinking patterns away from entrenched or predictable thinking to new or unexpected ideas.

A new idea that is the result of lateral thinking is not always a helpful one, but when a good idea is discovered in this way it is usually obvious in hindsight.

Edward de Bono points out that the term problem solving implies that there is a problem

to respond to and that it can be resolved. That eliminates situations where there is no problem, or a problem exists that cannot be resolved. It is logical to think about making a good situation, that has no problems, into a better situation. Sometimes a problem cannot be solved by removing its cause. **"We may need to solve problems not by removing the cause but by designing the way forward even if the cause remains in place."-Edward de Bono.**
Lateral thinking can be used to help in solving problems but can also be used to develop a new way of thinking even when there is no apparent problem.

It can identify latent opportunities. The late Earl Nightingale, in his audiotape series "The Essence of Success," suggests that when we're faced with a challenge that requires a creative solution, we should pursue both "horizontal" and "vertical" solutions. This creative problem-solving technique combines tried-and-true solutions with truly novel ideas, making a very effective tool in your personal ideation arsenal. **First, think vertically-** Vertical solutions are based on existing ideas or knowledge -- solutions that others have already had some success with.

To paraphrase Thomas Edison, the world outside of your industry, market or profession is full of existing ideas that people have never fully capitalized upon, which may be adapted to your specific need or challenge

When you're doing "vertical" research, Web search engines can help you to find articles, white papers, case histories and other documents that demonstrate how other people have tackled challenges like yours. Similarly, you can use online discussion forums to ask others for advice on how they solved a similar problem.

Thinking vertically is something like drilling deeper in an existing oil well or mining an existing seam in a gold mine that may already be just about tapped out. Digging deeper into known, familiar territory carries little risk, but is unlikely to result in a breakthrough idea.

Most of us tend to rely on safety and security of tried-and-true solutions -- the so-called conventional wisdom so typified by the expression, "That's the way it's always been done...". It takes courage to step out in a fresh, new direction.

Next, horizontal thinking- try thinking about your challenge horizontally -- in other words, come up with a variety of ideas by thinking in totally new directions. This is where creative

brainstorming techniques can be very useful. They whack you out of your familiar, rutted paths of thinking, and can help you to jump-start your thinking in new, creative directions
To use our oil drilling metaphor, vertical thinking is like digging exploratory wells in different locations, in hopes of finding new deposits of fresh, untapped ideas. Horizontal thinking tends to be riskier but is more likely to lead to a breakthrough idea. For example, replacing source of energy from oil to solar, powerful batteries (for electric cars), hybrid cars, fuel cell technology, bio fuel and so forth.

In real world problem-solving situations, a combination of both approaches usually produces the best results. This technique ensures that you tap the best existing ideas and information, while also generating novel, untested ideas, increasing the likelihood that you'll uncover the ideal solution to your problem or challenge

In fact, creativity experts suggest that you gather as much information as possible about your existing challenge or opportunity (vertical thinking) before you begin brainstorming novel solutions (horizontal thinking).

Breakthrough ideas like 3D printing in manufacturing will turn the industry upside down from high volume, low variety business to low volume (as small as 1), large, personalised variety of products, from subtractive process to additive process. Streaming video service companies like Netflix, Amazon Prime, Hotstar, Sling, Zee5, and others use the broad band to unleash a variety of content which the user can view at his time, convenience and choice, replacing dish, cable-based companies like Tata Sky, Airtel, Dish TV etc. Taxi companies, like Uber, Ola, Grab, Lyft and others, are providing ease of travel, and making car available on demand, giving the choice to us not to own a car or keep a driver. Drone based delivery services are waiting regulatory approval. Uber plans air taxi service by 2023 which will transform transportation using electrical vertical take-off and landing vehicles being developed by aircraft manufacturers.

<Exercise>
Can you join the Nine dots with four straight lines without lifting your pen.

If you succeed, try joining the dots with three straight lines without lifting the pen.

32
SCAMPER

SCAMPER is an acronym for a list of questions to generate improvements. It opens new ways of looking at things and generates innovative opportunities. Alex Osborn developed the list of questions that were later arranged as SCAMPER by Bob Eberle.

S	Substitute	What else can be done? Who else can participate? What materials can one substitute? What processes can one substitute? Another ingredient? Other material? Other process? Other power? Another place? Other approach? Other tone of voice? Other time?
C	Combine	How could ideas, features, solutions, perspectives be combined, blended, alloyed, made into a kit, an assortment, an ensemble?

A	Adapt, Adopt	How could one adapt other ideas, methods, systems, processes to this situation? What else is like the problem in hand? Does past offer parallel? What could I copy? Whom could I emulate?
M	Modify	Can one give a new feel, look, experience, taste? Can one change details? New twist? Change meaning, colour, motion, odour, taste, form, shape? Other changes?
	Magnify	What can be added? More time? Greater frequency? Stronger? Higher? Larger? Longer? Thicker? Heavier? Extra value? Plus, ingredient? Duplicate? Multiply? Exaggerate?
	Minify	Can it fit in smaller space? What to subtract? Smaller? Condensed? Miniature? Lower? Shorter? Narrower? Lighter? Omit? Streamline? Split up? Understate? Less frequent?

P	Put to other uses	Are there new ways to use as it is, new uses if modified? Will people benefit from new uses?
E	Eliminate	What items can be removed? What steps in working can be eliminated? What paper work can be eliminated?
R	Reverse	Can the order, sequence of work, be reversed, changed? What happens when one introduces opposites? Transpose positive and negative? Turn it backward, upside down, inside out? Reverse roles? Change shoes? Turn tables? Turn other cheek?
	Rearrange	What if the layout is changed? Can the sequence be changed? Can the components be interchanged? Another pattern? Another layout? Other sequence? Transpose cause and effect? Change place? Change schedule? Earlier? Later?

| | Reduce | Can steps of process/work be reduced? Can items be reduced? Can paperwork be reduced? |

Few other principles of improvement

- Concurrent processing-doing things in parallel, rather than serially, cuts lead time. down time.
- Prior preparation- keeping items ready ahead of the process.
- Simplification-moving from complex to simple design, using fewer parts.
- Sequencing-changing the order of doing.
- Using gravity for flow, saving energy.
- Using spring loading for providing force.
- Assigning right person for the job.
- Ergonomic design of workplace to reduce fatigue and improve efficiency.
- Reverse engineering- can be applied in the fields of mechanical engineering, electronics, software engineering and others to extract knowledge about the product design, architecture etc by studying existing object, and working backwards.
- Mechanisation-productivity improvement through mechanising operations being done

manually using, for example, powered hand tools, mechanised segregation/rejection system like vibratory screens, mechanised road building, railway track laying, etc

- Automation- technology which does not need human intervention or support using closed loop feedback control system for operating equipments and processes for manufacturing, quality, utilities and others. Most automation is computer controlled. PLCs (Programmable logic controllers) have replaced relay logic type systems. ATM is an example of automated banking.

Automation increasingly plays a major part in our daily lives like programmable thermostat allows us to run air conditioners and heaters more efficiently, programmable coffee maker sets the time to start brewing, easy bill paying options online saves the time of visiting utility bill and credit card companies which was needed few years before. Phone Apps have streamlined processes and added convenience. We also have Amazon's Alexa, which lets you voice control smart home devices such as lights, TVs, switches etc and can provide music, songs, all information like news, weather, sports, general knowledge, by just talking to Alexa.

33
Brainstorming

"It is easier to tone down a wild idea than to think up a new one."- Alex Osborn

Alex F Osborn is the father of brainstorming and pioneer in creative thinking. Brainstorming is done at every stage of problem solving. First for identifying problems in case the group is unable to find problems in their work area. Second for finding causes of the problem, and third for working out solutions. Whenever one gets stuck during problem solving, one should do brainstorming.

Brainstorming is a group or individual method of thinking up solutions, ideas or new concepts. As per Osborne who coined the word, brainstorm means using the **brain** to *storm* a creative problem and to do so "in commando fashion, each stormer audaciously attacking the same objective." Fear of failure, when solutions do not exist, and criticism from peers and seniors of their ideas, comes as a roadblock to effective brainstorming session. One should make it a rule that quantity of ideas is important in brainstorming, and not quality, and that no idea is stupid or ridiculous. All ideas are considered potentially good, and many times the innocuous or impractical looking idea turns out to be a winner. Analysis and evaluation of the idea should be done after the people have run out of ideas and the brainstorming session is over. This encourages creativity. If analysis and screening is done along with idea generation, the brain freezes, and it is unlikely that fresh ideas will emerge.

Structured brainstorming invariably generates creative ideas exploiting the brain's capacity for free thinking and lateral thinking. The brainstorming group has a facilitator and members. The facilitator starts the process, records ideas on board or flip chart, motivates people and encourages all persons in the group to speak out their mind. The facilitator follows few rules of brainstorming:

1. Group size between 6 to 10. If it is too large, participation is low, and many people remain in the background. If it is small, enough 'brain storm' is not created.
2. The facilitator should state the topic to be brainstormed and stay focused on the topic- it could be identification of problem, causes of problem, solutions to remove the root cause of problem.
3. Time limit to be set and should be between 20 to 40 minutes.

4. Quantity of ideas is important. The more the better. Brainstorming celebrates the maxim 'Quantity breeds Quality.'
5. Quality of ideas is not to be ascertained at this stage.
6. No criticism of ideas and no comments, verbal or non-verbal like 'this was tried earlier and failed,' 'this is theoretical,' 'this is not done anywhere,' 'I have thirty years of experience and never heard such stupidity,' and so forth.
7. Encourage wild, out of the box, weird and wacky ideas.
8. Build on each other's ideas by expanding, modifying, provoking, complementing, taking opposites etc. Encourage others to say "and" instead of "but."
9. Be visual. Use coloured markers, post it stickers, display ideas on wall, sketch your ideas, draw pictures.
10. Facilitate ease of communication and allow everyone to speak as well as listen to each other's ideas.
11. Conclude and thank the team members for their contribution.

Brainstorming is a group session. The siblings of brainstorming like braindumping will be an individual session, brainwriting and brain walking-both would be a combination of individual and group session. David Allen, author of *"Getting Things Done"* methodology, advocates braindump to free up mental energy and allow freethinking as holding your unexplored ideas, thoughts, unfinished tasks, creates mental blockages. Brain dump allows 'not so outspoken' persons to contribute actively.

Brainwriting is a good starting point for ideation session and can maximise the initial braindump. In brainwriting, participants write ideas onto cards or can mail them to other participants. One can also share them over a WhatsApp group. The participants build on each other's idea silently. The advantage is that there is no shouting like in a typical brainstorming session, and introverted people, who otherwise feel left out, can contribute.

Brainwalking is like brainwriting with one difference that participants move around, keeping their energy levels high and sharing their notes of ideas. Bryan Mattimore, a specialist in the art of ideation and facilitation, came up with this technique, and in his book *Idea Stormers*, he describes brainwalking as the: 'single best technique to use to begin an ideation session.'

34
TRIZ

TRIZ method of creative problem solving was developed by Russian inventor and science fiction writer Genrich Altshuller and is the Russian acronym for "Teoriya Resheniya Izobretatelskikh Zadatch" (теория решения изобретательских задач) which means "Theory of Inventive Problem Solving" (or TIPS). Altshuller reviewed about 40000 patents and looked for patterns and clues for understanding how innovation took place. He found there was a method in the madness of creation and wrote in 1969 the book "Algorithm for Inventing." He proposed a set of 40 principles which can be used for problem solving for a variety of problems.

The 40 principles were based on Six pillars.
Six Pillars of TRIZ:
1. **Concept of Technical System**s

   Technical system is an integration of inputs, processes and outputs which fulfils the desired tasks and objective. It consists of subsystems in hierarchical structure till the lowest element. Each element and sub system has a life after which it is upgraded and revised. When solving problems, innovators study the technical system and think improvements.

2. Levels of Innovation

Level 1: Simple improvements made with knowledge and resources available within the system of the organisation.

Level 2: Inputs from systems of similar organisations are needed.

Level 3: Knowledge from other organisations and branches of science is needed.

Level 4: Innovation from different fields are used.

Level 5: Replacement by new technology or disruptive innovation.

Altshuller found that first two levels contributed to 77% of solutions.

3. Concept of Contradiction

Problem requires an innovative solution when improving one parameter impacts negatively on another. For example, use of higher gauge material improves strength but increases weight of the system. For take-off and landing on the runway, aircraft needs wheels but when in the air, the wheels are a drag. Retracting the wheels after take-off resolves the conflict.

The best solutions come when the contradiction is resolved.

4. Ideal

The pursuit of the innovator must be the ideal result for the user or the customer.

5. Use of Resources

Resources to be considered are Space, People, Time, Energy, Knowledge, Information, System resources, Substance resources, Harmful substances. These are available within the system but hidden and needs the insights of the problem solver to uncover. For example, shortage of space in warehouse is a problem, but utilising vertical space was not considered as a solution because vertical racking and high-rise material handling equipments were not thought of. Snake poison is used as an antidote for snake bite. When short of manpower, going for self-service, as in restaurants, is innovative. Making use of time, while machine is running, as in SMED (single minute exchange of dies), helps to lower the total cycle time. Using waste energy of furnace for generating power for captive use saves precious fuel. Widening the applications of existing system software, increasing knowledge base by developing a knowledge bank internally for sharing of information, are ways of maximising use of resources. Sinter plant in steel industry uses every bit of waste like coal fines, iron ore fines, lime dust etc. and thereby lowers cost.

6. Patterns of Evolution

Altshuller observed that same type of patterns are repeated in evolution of systems.

- Uneven evolution of systems.

  Some develop faster, some lag. Hardware development in computer industry has led to development of software in a bigger way, to the extent they become 'hardware hungry'. Good roads motivate car producers for better cars and higher production, which the roads in many developing countries are not able to cope with.

- Transition to micro level.

  System is divided into smaller units. Examples are miniaturised circuits, SBUs in management, mist spray in taps to conserve water, smaller states.

- Transition to macro level.

  Functions are combined, divisions are merged to become larger and bigger. This is the opposite of above. Examples of large capacity super thermal power plants, integrated steel

plants, larger capacities to make use of economies of scale, mergers of companies and their divisions, large size TV screens etc.

- Increase of interactions.

  Addition of material, system, to make the primary system more effective.

  For example, adding plastic chips in road building increases the life of roads. Addition of spare parts in human body like tooth implant, stent, heart valve etc.

- Expansion and convolution, trimming.

  As systems evolve, they become bigger, more elements and sub systems get added to it making it unwieldy and inefficient. Then the process of simplification, removing items, trimming parts starts. For example, reduction of manpower, cost cutting initiatives, simplifying design, removing clutter, making things lighter etc. Landline system with big cable network and hordes of linesmen, replaced in a major way by mobile, wireless network.

40 inventive principles of problem solving using TRIZ

1. Segmentation (Fragmentation)

Modular furniture, truck and trailer instead of one large truck. Venetian blinds instead of solid shades.

2. Separation (taking out, extraction)

Split air-conditioner-noisy compressor outside the room and quite blower in the room.

3. Local quality.

Change the object's structure from uniform to non-uniform, change external environment from uniform to non-uniform or influence-use pressure, density, temperature gradient. Make each part of object function in conditions most suitable for its operation-tiffin box with separate compartments. Make each part of an object fulfil different function-pencil with eraser, phone with torch, hammer with nail puller. Separate products like biscuits, soap, toothpaste, for urban and rural market needs.

4. Symmetry change

Asymmetrical vanes in symmetrical vessels like concrete mixers, blenders, improves mixing.

5. Merging (consolidation)

Many functions combined in cell phones, networked computers, merging of companies.

6. Multifunctionality (universality)

Phone with voice recorder. Multitasking by people in organisation.

7. "Nested doll" (nesting)

Place one object inside another-coffee cups. Make one-part pass through a cavity in other- seat belt retraction mechanism, zoom lens.

8. Weight compensation (anti-weight, counterweight)

Air tanks in submarines. Providing traction to exercise muscles. Road barriers.

9. Preliminary counter action (prior counter action)

Masking before harmful exposure (X rays). Masking tape to prevent area not being painted.

10. Preliminary action (prior action, do it in advance)

Keeping material ready in location before start of set up in machine. Keeping all sterilised surgical instruments in sealed tray before start of surgery. Prior arrangements of tyre change, fuel filling, check and positioning crew at pit stop in formula one car racing.

11. Beforehand compensation (beforehand cushioning, cushion in advance)

Prepare for emergency measures or improve detection to compensate for the relatively low reliability of the object, like smoke detector, leaking gas detector and automatic shut off.

12. Equipotentiality (bring things to the same level)

Change of operating conditions to avoid working against a potential field like gravity or a magnetic field, like spring loaded parts delivery or gravity flow through chutes.

13. "The other way around" (do it in reverse, do it inversely)

Invert the actions used to solve the problem - cooling instead of heating or vice versa. Make movable parts fixed and fixed parts movable- treadmill (for walking or running in place), rotate the part instead of the tool. Turning an object upside down to fix screws, to unload.

14. Spheroidality-Curvature increase

Move from flat to spherical surface, from rectilinear to curvilinear-use of arches and domes for strength in buildings. Ball point and roller point pens for smooth ink distribution. Change from linear to rotary motion-spinning clothes in washing machine.

15. Dynamics

Allow the characteristics of an object, environment or process to change for optimal benefit, like dynamic pricing by airlines and taxi services like Uber, adjustable seats, adjustable mirrors, tool cupboard on wheels so that it can be moved to position where required.

16. Partial or excessive actions

If 100% of the desired outcome is difficult, using slightly less or slightly more of the same method may make it easier to solve the problem. For example, over spray when painting and then remove excess paint, or do test marketing in limited segments before full market launch.

17. Dimensionality change

Move an object in multi-dimensional space- multi axis cutting tools. Use a multi-storey arrangement of objects instead of a single storey, for instance, multi-storeyed parking lot. Tilt or reorient the object-dump truck. Use another side of a given area- electronic chips on both sides of printed circuit board.

18. Mechanical vibration (including piezo electric, ultrasound, electromagnetic field vibration)

Make an object vibrate, oscillate, increase its frequency. Examples are many like vibratory feeder for feeding material, high frequency sound waves for destroying gall stones or kidney stones, alert for calls and messages in mobile phones.

19. Periodic action

Instead of continuous action, use periodic or pulsating action, change frequency or use pauses between impulses. For example, industrial sirens, warning beeps, light signals.

20. Continuity of useful action

Carry on work continuously like use of flywheel or hydraulic system for storing energy, elimination of idle portions like printing during return of the printer carriage.

21. Hurrying (skipping, rushing through)

Conduct a process at high speed-dentist drill at high speed to avoid heating, cutting plastic at high speed to avoid deformation, short pulses of laser to do micro surgery of the eye.

22. Blessing in disguise (convert harm into benefit)

Electric spark erodes metal-this principle is used in spark erosion machine to cut metal for making intricate parts. In vaccination, small doses of harmful viruses are injected, and the body develops antibodies to combat the virus. Waste heat can be used for generating power, scrap can be recycled, creating fire in opposite direction to extinguish forest fire.

23. Feedback

Automatic control systems in equipments, plant, home equipments like geysers, ovens, and customer feedback for improvement in product and systems.

24. Intermediary

Use of an intermediary object or process like jigs and fixtures for locating and positioning jobs, pot holder to carry hot dishes to the dining table.

25. Self service

Make an object or system serve itself and perform auxiliary functions. For example, self-check kits for blood pressure and sugar levels, self service restaurants, animal waste as fertiliser, food waste to create compost.

26. Copying

Use simpler and inexpensive copies in place of expensive, fragile and difficult to obtain objects. For instance, computer simulated pilot training instead of actual flight, video conference instead of physical presence, scanned copies instead of originals, thermal imaging to detect overheating of wires in electrical panels, sonography to detect health of foetus.

27. Cheap disposables

Replace permanent objects with disposable objects like disposable syringes for injections, disposable plates and cups, disposable diapers and temporary manpower.

28. Mechanical substitution

Replacement of mechanical sensors or objects with electronic, optical sensors and microprocessor-based objects using artificial intelligence and robotics.

29. Pneumatics and hydraulics

Use gas and liquid in objects like shoe sole inserts, air mattresses, air curtains at entrance of dust free rooms, inflatable boats and beds and pillows, hydraulic system for storing energy during deceleration of vehicle to be used later during acceleration.

30. Flexible shells and thin films

Thin walled throw away plastic containers instead of glass bottles for mineral water, soft drinks and juices.

31. Porous materials

Floor mops with special porous material that absorbs water on the floor easily, which is later squeezed out, drilling holes in structure to reduce weight, porosity of earthen pot hastens evaporation and keeps water cool.

32. Colour changes

Standard colour codes for identifying fluid (water-hot, cold, waste, gas-oxygen, nitrogen, LPG etc, oil, steam) flowing through pipes, identifying cables and wires, identifying grades of steel etc. Fluorescent lights for road and traffic indications, colour additives to track the flow of liquids in a system including human body, packing in transparent packets for visibility.

33. Homogeneity

Objects interacting with the main object should be of similar material as the main object. For example, ice cream cones are edible, paper wrapping for burgers which are microwave friendly and can be heated together, diamond cutting tool out of diamonds, etc

34. Discarding and recovering

Get rid of portions of an object that have fulfilled their function by discarding, dissolving, evaporating or modifying. Like multistage rockets hauled in space for putting a satellite in orbit are discarded after fulfilling their function; using sulphuric acid, hydrochloric acid in detergents industry and then recovering spent acid which is used in fertilisers; dissolving gelatine capsule for medicine.

35. Parameter changes

Change of physical state-solid, liquid, gas; change of concentration or density; change of degree of flexibility; change of temperature, volume. Cooking gas is stored and transported in cylinders as liquid; vulcanised rubber has more durability; increase in cooking temperature changes taste, texture and aroma.

36. Phase transitions

The phenomena of change during phase transition is used, for example, in air conditioning and refrigeration, when state changes from liquid to gas, cooling takes place.

37. Thermal expansion (or contraction)

Bimetal thermostat uses metals of two different coefficients of thermal expansion. Fitment of a steel tyre over a wheel is done by heating the tyre and slipping it over the wheel, so that when it cools down it has shrunk fit

38. Strong oxidants

Use of oxygen to produce steel by injecting it into the electric arc furnace with hot metal from blast furnace thus avoiding or minimising use of electrodes and saving power. Air is ionised to trap pollutants in air cleaner. Oxygen is used to bleach paper.

39. Inert atmosphere

Many metals like aluminium are welded in an inert argon atmosphere to reduce oxidation of welded parts. Bio digesters in railway toilets use bacteria which flourish in anaerobic environment. Inert atmosphere in heat treatment furnace to prevent decarburisation.

40. Composite materials

Change from uniform to composite materials like reinforced concrete, glass fibre reinforced plastics, ink with magnetic material used in

MICR (magnetic ink character recognition), composite epoxy resin/carbon fibre golf club shafts, aircraft parts etc which are lighter.

Managing contradictions

Systems evolve towards ideality by overcoming contradictions. A contradiction is a simple clash of solutions. For example, production head wants enough inventory of material so that there is no stoppage of production for want of material, but the finance head wants minimum inventory to cut down the financial cost of carrying inventory. The production unit prefers large batch sizes so that frequent set ups and changeovers are not needed, but customers want variety and sales team gets small quantity orders for varied grades and types of product.

TRIZ contradiction matrix of 39 characteristics of systems applies the 40 principles to solve these contradictions. Concept of contradiction is central to TRIZ method of problem solving. New ideas are generated by resolving contradictions faced when designing a product or system.

Contradiction Matrix for Problem Solving

Improve this ↓	Parameters	1	2	3	4	5	6	....	39
Technical Contradictions	1								
	2								
	3								
	4								
	5								
	6								
	...								
	39								

(Without making this worse →)

The contradiction matrix is a 39X39 matrix which has 39 Technical characteristics which one wants to improve on one side, without worsening the same 39 parameters on the other side. The 39 factors are as under:

1	Weight of moving object
2	Weight of stationary object
3	Length of moving object
4	Length of stationary object
5	Area of moving object
6	Area of stationary object
7	Volume of moving object
8	Volume of stationary object
9	Speed
10	Force (intensity)

11	Stress or pressure
12	Shape
13	Stability of the object's composition
14	Strength
15	Duration of action of moving object
16	Duration of action by stationary object
17	Temperature
18	Illumination density
19	Use of energy by moving object
20	Use of energy by stationary object
21	Power
22	Loss of energy
23	Loss of substance
24	Loss of information
25	Loss of time
26	Quantity of substance/the matter
27	Reliability
28	Measurement accuracy
29	Manufacturing precision
30	Object-affected harmful factors
31	Object-generated harmful factors
32	Ease of manufacture
33	Ease of operation
34	Ease of repair
35	Adaptability or versatility
36	Device complexity
37	Difficulty of detecting and measuring
38	Extent of automation
39	Productivity/Capacity

35
Kaizen

Kaizen is incremental and continual improvement through elimination of waste. It is a Japanese way of improvement and evolving a quality culture involving all people. It is a combination of Kai meaning to modify and change, and Zen meaning to think, to make good and better.

Wherever there is a method or process, there is an opportunity for doing it in a better way.

Any work which does not add Value, that takes one away from one's goal, is a Waste. It could be excess movement, transportation, inventory, defects-scrap, rejects, customer returns, rework, waiting-delays, idling, stoppages, extra processing, bad system or method, low speed, lack of plan, unutilised people's creativity, line imbalance, strain, large variation, uneven output, excess paperwork, system downtime etc.

The heart of Kaizen is rotating the PDCA cycle and standardising after every stage of improvement, then improving the plan and repeating PDCA. Continuously doing PDCA brings progress.

Plan (P)-formulate and define the problem and think countermeasures using various problem-solving tools. Do (D)-execute the plan. Check (C) – whether things happened as per plan. Action (A) – modify or improve the plan.

> **Kaizen is the umbrella for all improvement processes and tools covered in this book.**

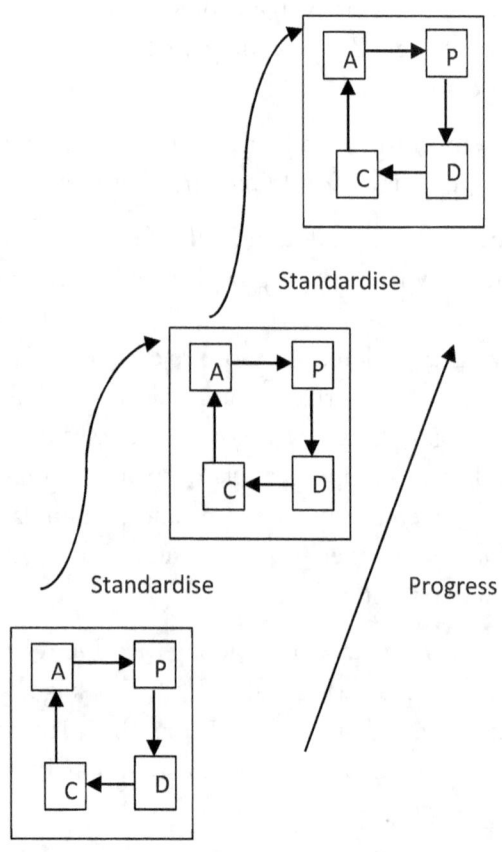

If plan is successful, standardise it and go for an improved plan, and continue with iterations and increase in challenging goals.

PDCA and Problem Solving

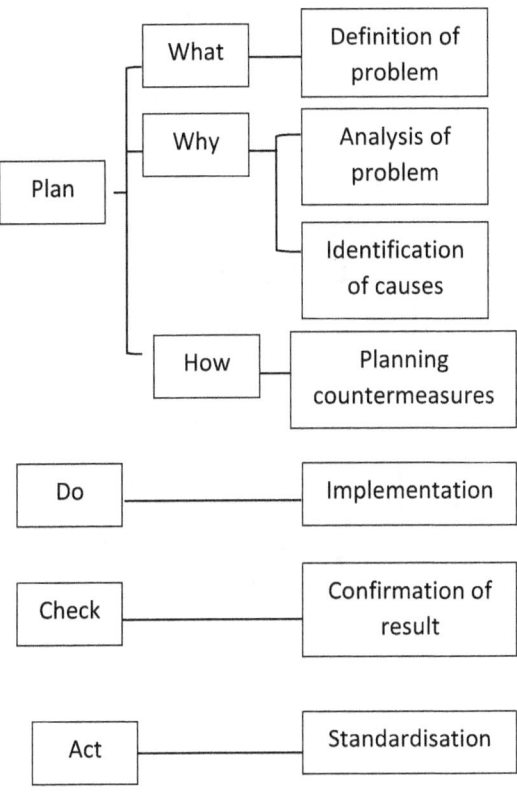

Control

36
Standardise

"Standard work sheets and the information contained in them are important elements of the Toyota Production System. For a production person to be able to write a standard work sheet that other workers can understand, he or she must be convinced of its importance.... High production efficiency has been maintained by preventing the recurrence of defective products, operational mistakes, and accidents, and by incorporating workers' ideas. All of this is possible because of the innocuous work sheet" .... Taiichi Ohno, founder of Toyota Production System.

Today's standardisation is the baseline on which tomorrow's improvement will be based. Standardisation must be thought of as the best we can do today but which will be improved tomorrow. Such a thought process leads to progress. If we get comfortable on achieving a standard, or if we think standards confine creativity, we will stop all progress.

Standardised work in manufacturing consists of three elements-takt time (time required to complete one job at the pace of customer demand), the sequence of doing things or sequence of processes, and how much inventory the unit station needs to have to achieve the standard work. These are written down and displayed as SOP (Standard operating process/procedure) and work sheets.

One needs to find the correct balance between the rigid procedure which people must follow and the freedom to innovate and solve problems. The standards have to be specific, yet general enough to allow for flexibility in terms of revisions and updates. Standards have to be the foundation for continuous improvement.

An enabling environment for problem solving and innovation must be created. Bureaucracy is efficient when technology is not changing, and environment is stable. Coercive bureaucracy uses standards to control people, reprimand them breaking rules and create fear to bring them on track. Enabling system uses the best practice methods, designed and improved upon with the participation of people, and standards help people to control their own work.

To remain competitive continually among leaders, one must have viable and enabling standards, and a harmonious balance between a task and people-oriented organization.

		Social Structure	
Technical Structure	**High Bureaucracy**	**Coercive Bureaucracy** • Rigid rule enforcement • Extensive written rules, procedures and protocols • Hierarchy controls	**Enabling bureaucracy** • Empowered employees • Rules & procedures as enabling tools • Hierarchy supports organisational learning
	Low bureaucracy	**Autocratic** • Top down control • Minimum written rules and procedures • Hierarchy controls	**Organic** • Empowered employees • Minimum rules and procedures • Little hierarchy

Source: The Toyota Way, adapted from P.S.Adler, "Building better bureaucracies".

<Example of SOP>

SOP for writing a book
1. Purpose   To serve as a guide for budding writers
2. Process Owner   The author of the book
3. Support Processes   Page layout and formatting, Designing cover and inner pages, Editing, Proof reading, Visual aids
4. Performance Indicators   Error free regarding grammar, spelling, formatting. Published on time, Good feedback
5. Process
5.1 Process Inputs   The source of information and references
5.2 Process Steps   Ideation- theme of book, what the book is about   Broad outline of content   Developing content   Making notes, drafting text   Revising and editing   Making pdf   Publishing-printing, binding, distribution
5.3 Process Output   Published and printed book in desired copies
6. Process Monitoring and Measurement   Time schedule   Quality-cover design, content, inner design, binding, printing
7. Resources   Laptop, voice recorder, page designer, Illustrator, proof reader, publishing software
8. Reference documents and records   About author, past books, bibliography, acknowledgements.

<Example of Work Sheet/Work Instructions>

Work Sheet for making tea
Responsibility   Host
Product   Tea, one quality of tea as a standard. Variety not on offer.
Instructions
1. Estimate number of people who will take tea.
2. Estimate milk, tea leaves, water, sugar requirement based on number of people taking tea.
3. Prior preparation: keep sugar, tea leaves, spoon, strainer, kettle, cups ready.
4. Fill kettle with desired quantity of water.
5. Start gas burner and put the kettle on gas. Let it heat up.
6. When water begins to boil, pour tea leaves of required quantity, stir with spoon and switch off the gas.
7. Allow tea to brew for two minutes
8. Pour tea on cups. Keep milk and sugar in separate pots. Guests can add them as per their choice.
9. Serve the guests on a tray
10. Take feedback

37
Control sheets
Check sheets

To ensure that the solution to the problem is sustainable and is providing the stated benefits, control measures like check sheet, control sheet, should be used.

We have already discussed the template and content of check sheets in earlier chapter.

<Examples>

1. Inventory control sheet in warehouse- this keeps track of inventory, SKUs (stock keeping units), non-moving items vis a vis target. If the problem was shortage of warehouse space, and the solution was to reduce SKUs and finished goods inventory, control of this parameter is critical.
2. Customer despatch control sheet- how much has been despatched and how much should have been. If the gap is large, it implies problems of production, logistics-trucks not getting arranged, or cash crunch, have not been resolved.

3. Packing check sheet-a comprehensive packing list ensures that items are not missed out during despatch. A customer is really annoyed when he finds nuts and bolts, foundation bolts or stoppers etc missing in his large consignment as he cannot use or install it without these items.
4. Inspection check sheet-this gives the confidence that all items as per quality standards have been checked and is prepared for various stages of manufacturing, assembly and despatch.
5. Cleaning check sheet
   What all to clean, where to clean, what time to clean – this gets covered in a cleaning check sheet which is helpful in monitoring and control
6. Lubrication check sheet
   One major reason for equipment breakdowns is insufficient or wrong lubrication. A lubrication check sheet will be a reminder on what to lubricate, when, how and with what lubricant in how much quantity.

More Problem-Solving Approaches

38
Theory of Constraints

The Theory of Constraints (TOC) as a management philosophy, developed by Dr. E. M. Goldratt, recognizes that organizations exist to achieve a goal but are limited in their ability to achieve the goal by the "constraint" factor. Businesses need to identify and manage constraints. Identification of constraints requires a focused approach, and the constraints may not be apparent, for instance, they could be hidden under 'company's policy.' The analogy of a chain, where its strength depends on its weakest link, is true in all organisations where the weakest link or the "bottleneck" decides the pace of the line.

TOC says that management needs to find the weak link in the chain and strengthen the weakest link-the constraint, thereby increasing the chain strength.

The goal of a business organisation is to make more money by increasing throughput, which gets converted to sales, and reducing inventory and operating expenses. The goal of a non-commercial organisation would be to increase people happiness by increasing throughput of high quality, service at affordable price and reducing expenses.

The Five focusing steps of TOC are:

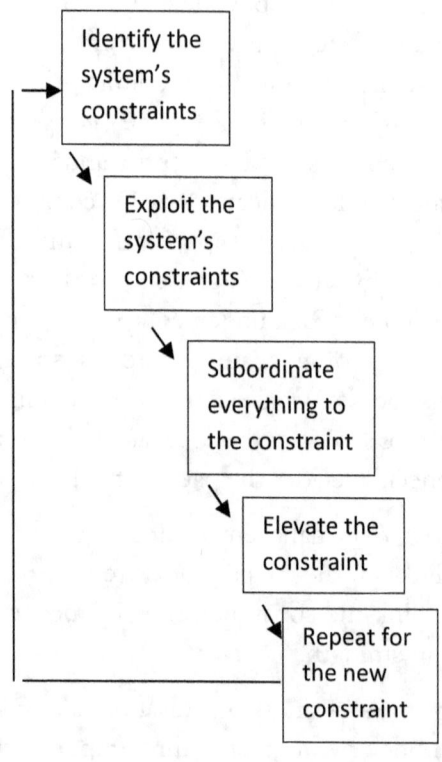

\<Example\>

Goal: Increase rate of despatch from warehouse

Warehouse in charge is unable to fulfil the goal. The reason given- Space limitation because of which he is unable to organise the warehouse and consequently searching and retrieving items was taking considerable time, delaying despatches.

The expressed constraint: Space

Was space really the constraint? Close investigation and physical study of the warehouse revealed that 80% of space was occupied by non-moving SKUs (stock keeping units). Marketing was asked to clear the non-moving SKUs at discounted price, and warehouse team organised the remaining SKUs in designated locations with clear marking and accessibility.

Going by steps of TOC:

1. Identify system's constraints- space shortage because of excess SKUs, non-moving SKUs
2. Exploit the system's constraint- clear non-moving SKUs, optimise product mix for future, use vertical space for

storage, marketing to formulate strategy for SKUs
3. Subordinate everything to the constraint- Production to produce only what Marketing instructs, no less no more. Should avoid overproduction just to keep the production line busy.
4. Elevate the constraint-with free space available, the stocking will be efficient and despatch faster. Go for stacking vertically, use pallets, use high rise fork lifts, computerise warehouse stock inventory so that all details including location are known, and train people for quick search and retrieval.

   But now a new constraint has emerged- the non- availability of trucks.
5. Repeat for the new constraint-truck non-availability.

39

Business Process Reengineering

Reengineering is the fundamental rethinking and radical redesign of business processes to achieve dramatic improvements in critical measures of performance such as cost, quality, service, and speed.

1. Fundamental:

- Why do we do what we do? Why do we do it the way we do? What a company must do? It must focus on its core strengths. However, it should not outsource the core processes, as it will then lose its competitive advantage.
- 'What should be' the process and not 'what is'. Take nothing for granted.

2. Radical:

- Getting to the root of things- no superficial changes. Throwing away the old structures and procedures.

3. Dramatic

- Not marginal improvements but quantum leaps in performance.

4. Processes

Business process – a collection of activities that take one or more kinds of inputs and creates an output that is of value to the customer.

Re-engineering is reviewing the methods of performing the existing operations from zero base and rearranging the business process itself.

1. Zero base: Considering something totally afresh from a blank state without getting influenced by the past results or traditions.

Planning a budget for new year without referring to previous year and starting with zero base is called as zero-base budget.

2. Degree of customer satisfaction (CS): increase in sales through improvement in CS.

3. Overall optimisation: a way of thinking which supports any activity provided it brings in a total benefit for the enterprise, even if some sections face a loss.

Move from partial optimisation to holistic and total optimisation.

4. World class performance. Re-engineering is not simple improvement but a reform activity to bring about 'best in the world' results.

Process approach versus function approach

Most of us work in a functional silo, and our objective is limited to fulfilling the functional role. Typical functional mindset is 'My work extends from this place to this place.' "This is not my business."

<Example> Marketing is a function. Service is a function. Front office is a function. Accounts is a function. Now suppose a call comes to the front office from a customer wanting some repair work in his washing machine. The flow of work as per functional approach will be as follows:

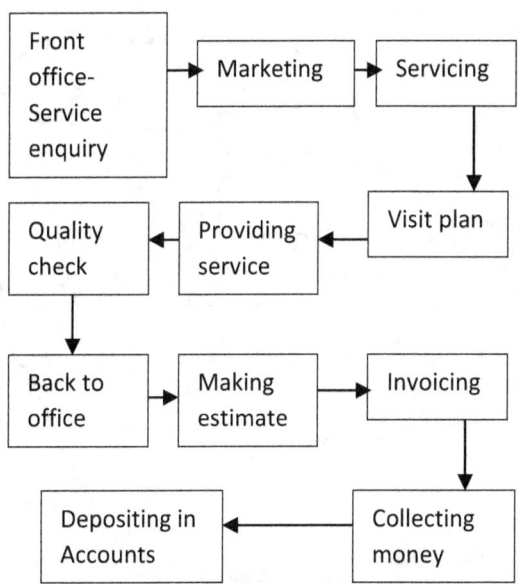

Such a way of doing work is bound to annoy the customer as there will be delays, people will not be available and the response to service will be poor.

Any work in an enterprise is composed of a flow of processes. Reforms should be carried out process wise and not function wise. In the above example, the goal is to provide prompt service. The process approach would direct the call to Servicing and they will visit, do the repair, raise the invoice and collect money, all at one time, and deposit the money in accounts.

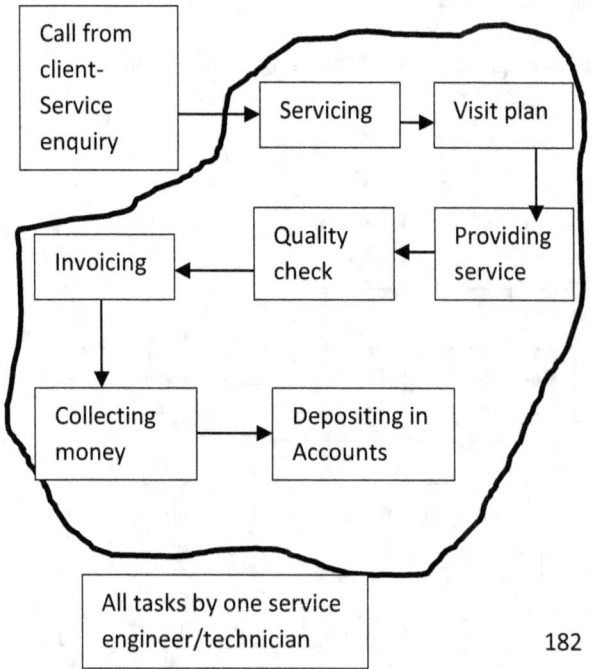

Process map may show time lines, Value and Non-value adding tasks and processes, and the responsible person. Process map to be made for 'As Is' situation and then after identifying problems and thinking improvements, a 'To Be' process map is prepared.

Division of work

Abolish division of work, as beyond a necessary level, division of work results in waste since it does not generate added value. This is possible by promoting delegation of powers, combining or merging closely related processes, formation of flat organisation and delayering which also improves communication and reduces cost, forming self-empowered teams, eliminating duplicacy of work and reducing middle level managerial manpower.

Reduce cycle time

Cycle time is the period from start till end of operation. Reduction of cycle time brings down cost, shortens response time to client's enquiry, and reduces delivery period giving the organisation a competitive edge. BPR aims at shortening of cycle time for development period, and for all stages from product planning to sales, by reducing handoff/catch ball operations, using technology and various techniques for time reduction.

<Example> United Colours of Benetton
Before situation

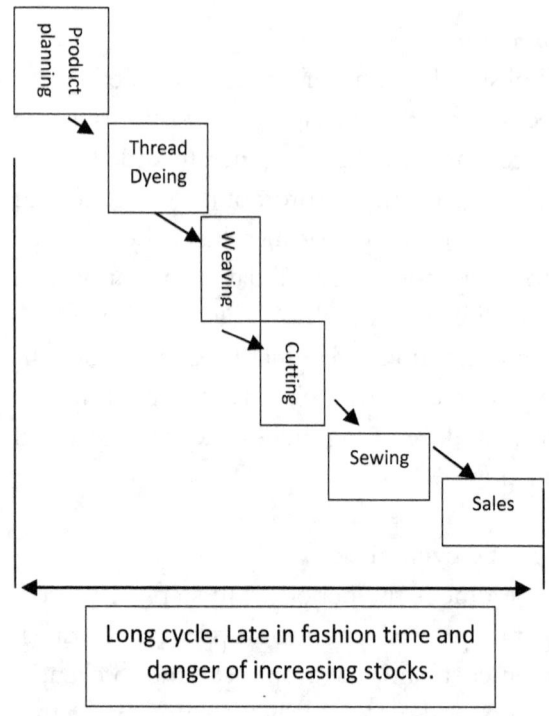

Long cycle. Late in fashion time and danger of increasing stocks.

<Example> United Colours of Benetton
After situation

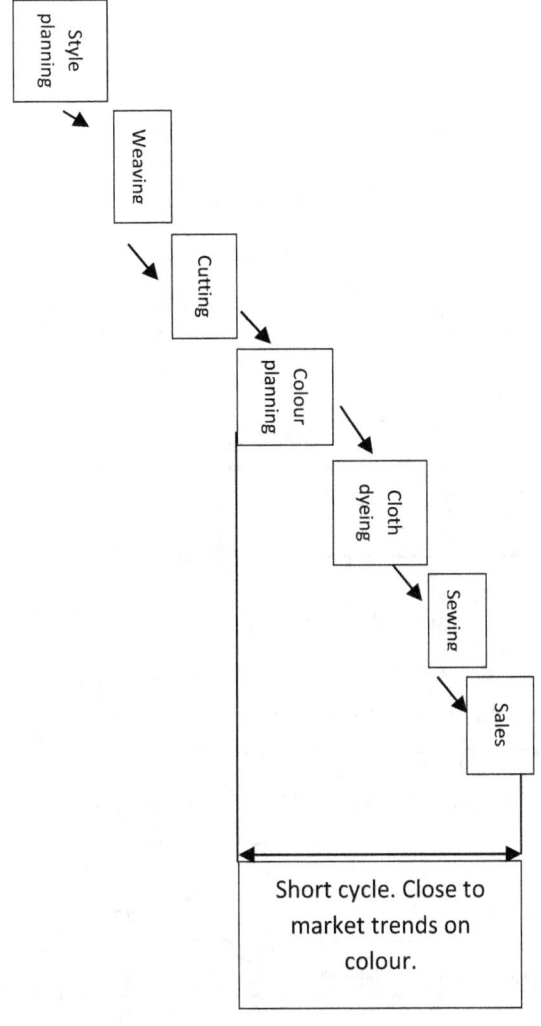

Distribute the work

Instead of carrying work in centralized manner, distribute it closer to where it is needed. For example, decentralize maintenance, servicing, grievance and complaints handling etc. to improve response and service.

Concurrent execution of jobs

1. Running jobs in parallel instead of serially to save time. T2 is less than T1

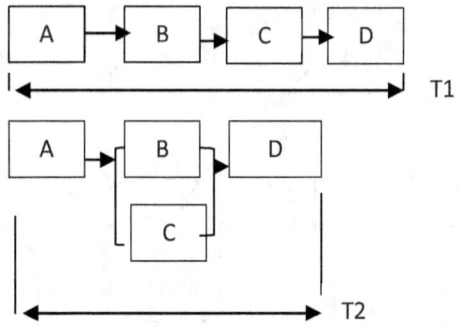

2. Synchronising jobs

B starts immediately after A, and C after B.

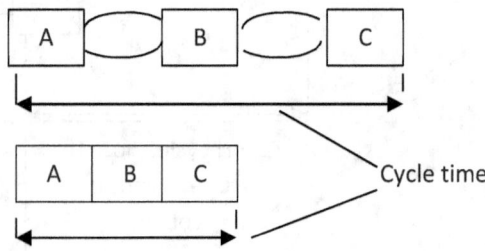

3. Overlapping jobs

The second job starts before the first one is finished as one sees in a relay race. This cuts down cycle time further.

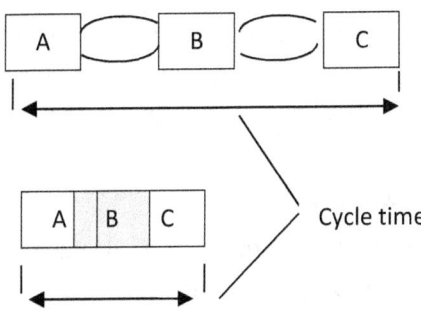

Cycle time

4. Abolishing division of labour

Combining A, B, C and D's work into one person's job.

For example, the receptionist does the job of receiving calls, scheduling appointments, photocopying- scanning- printing, and front office supervision.

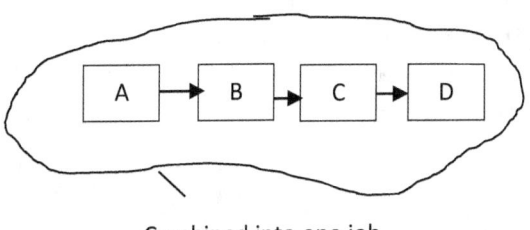

Combined into one job

Abolishing jobs considered obvious so far
Review from the viewpoint that they may not be necessary. Jobs like supervision, adjustment, inspection etc. need to be reviewed from value adding point of view and minimised. Self-certified vendors for 'A' category products do not require inspection. Improving processes, design and equipment can minimise the need to have a huge quality control department of inspectors.

Empowerment
Once empowerment has been carried out, the person does not act on behalf of somebody, but he rather makes all the decisions on his own initiative. In an assembly line, workers should be empowered to stop the line if they see a problem. In hotels, employees at the junior most level must be empowered to take actions on the spot for satisfying customers when the situation is such that they cannot wait for instructions from their seniors. The jurisdiction of people expands like a flat organisation.

The success stories must be shared, and failures must be appreciated, to build a sound culture of empowerment.

40
Six Sigma

The six sigma approach was first introduced and developed at Motorola in early 1990s. Credit for coining the term "Six Sigma," a federally registered trademark of Motorola, goes to a Motorola engineer named Bill Smith who worked under initiative of Bob Galvin, Chairman of Motorola. Later in the mid-nineties it was adopted by GE and Allied Signal. According to Jack Welch, ex CEO of GE, 'Six Sigma is the most challenging and potentially rewarding strategy GE has ever undertaken.'

Six Sigma quality level is 3.4 ppm (parts per million) or 99.9997% perfect. A 2% quality level, which was the acceptable quality level (AQL) in recent past, is 20000 ppm, and way away from the six sigma target for world class performance. Six sigma is customer focused, top driven business strategy, using process approach, facts and data and a statistical based quality metric.

Sigma is a Greek word used to describe variability. In statistical quality control, this means "standard deviation" (σ for population, and s for sampling distribution), which is a measure of dispersion around the mean.

$$s = \sqrt{\frac{\sum(x_i - \bar{x})^2}{n-1}}$$

The six-sigma approach should be used when the answers to following three questions are as under:

1. Is there a problem or opportunity?...both
2. Is the cause of the problem known?...No
3. Is the solution obvious?................No

Sigma level	DPMO	COQ as % of sales
2	308537	too high!
3	66807	25-40%
4	6210	15-25%
5	233	5-15%
6	3.4	less then 1%

DPMO-defect per million opportunities

COQ- Cost of Quality

The highest quality producer is also the lowest cost producer.

Six sigma follows the **DMAIC** approach to problem solving.

Define (D)

What is the business affecting problem?

Identify the customer, Prepare high level process map, Define scope of project, resource requirements, due date, and deliverables.

Measure (M)

What are the metrics? How is measurement done? Are measurements reliable? Is data available? How do we measure progress and success of the project?

Analyse (A)

Analyse process flow, define handoffs, develop and validate hypothesis, root cause analysis.

Improve (I)

Develop ideas to remove root cause, implement solutions, test results, standardise.

Control (C)

Document process, check points to control performance.

Tools for DMAIC

Define	Voice of customer, Brainstorming, SIPOC diagram (process map - S Supplier, I Input, P Process steps, O Output, C Customer), Benchmarking, Pareto diagram, Project tracking, Customer satisfaction survey.
Measure	Metrics and data sheet on yield, quality, breakdowns etc, Process capability indices Cp and Cpk, OEE (Overall equipment effectiveness), sigma level, mean and sigma, benchmarking.
Analyse	Distribution-mean, sigma, histogram, distribution graph; Pareto analysis, graphs, scatter diagram, check sheets, control charts, cause and effect or fish bone diagram, why..why and 6W2H analysis, root cause analysis, regression analysis, hypothesis testing, design of experiments, ANOVA.

Improve	Kaizen, technology, poka yoke, six thinking hats, lateral thinking, brainstorming.
Control	Statistical Process Control, Visual controls, project tracking, control sheets and check sheets.

For doing a successful six sigma project, the person leading the team must show leadership, positive mindset, good knowledge of advanced statistics, and must have good project management, and technical skills.

In six sigma, a technical problem is formulated as a statistical problem, for which statistical solution is found, which has to be then converted into a technical solution. For example, noise coming from car may be because of many variables. The statistical study will identify variables which are most significant contributors to the noise. It is then for the technical team to find solutions for elimination of the bad effects of identified variables.

41
Process Capability Studies

In planning the quality aspects of manufacture, nothing is more important than advance assurance that the process will be able to hold the tolerances. Process capability provides a quantified prediction of process adequacy. Process capability is the measured, inherent variation of the product turned out by a process. Process capability = $\pm 3\sigma$ (a total of 6σ) where σ is the standard deviation of the process under a state of statistical control, that is, under no drift and no sudden changes.

If the process is centered at the nominal specification and follows a normal distribution, 99.73% of production will fall within $\pm 3\sigma$ of the nominal specification.

Process capability depends on technology, equipment precision and reliability, degree of automation, processes, training and experience of personnel and so forth.

Relationship of Process Capability to Product Tolerance

A major reason for quantifying process capability is to be able to compute the ability of the process to hold product tolerances.

C_p = Capability ratio = Specification range/ Process Capability

$$= (USL - LSL)/6\sigma$$

where USL is the upper specification limit and LSL is the lower specification limit.

The process capability as measured by C_p refers to the variation in a process about the average value. This is illustrated in Fig. The two processes have equal capabilities C_p because 6σ is the same for each distribution.

The process aimed at μ_2 is producing defectives because the aim is off center, not because of the inherent variation about the aim (that is, the capability).

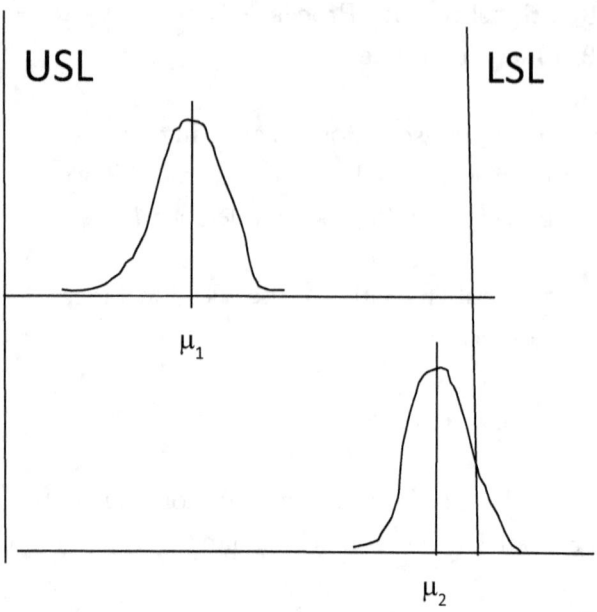

The higher the value of C_{pk}, lower will be the amount of product which is outside the specification limits. In certifying suppliers, most organisations use C_{pk} as one element of certifying criteria.

C_{pk} reflects the current process mean's proximity to either the USL or LSL.

$C_{pk} = \min\,[\,(X - LSL)/3s,\,(USL - X)/3s\,]$

Only absolute values are considered (ignore signs). s is an estimate of σ.

Some Examples Of Process Variability

Process	C_p	Total outside limits	Typical action to be taken
	< 1.0	≥ 5.0%	Heavy process control, sorting, rework etc.
	1.0	0.3%	Heavy process control, inspection
	1.33	64ppm	Reduced inspection, selected use of control charts
	1.63	1 ppm	Spot checking, selected use of control charts

The C_p index measures potential capability assuming that the process average is equal to the midpoint of the specification limits and the process is operating in statistical control

As the average is often not at the midpoint, it is useful to have a capability index that reflects both variation and the location of the process average. Such an index is C_{pk}.

42
Lean Management

Henry Ford, the founder of the Ford Motor Company, and development of assembly line technique for mass production which reduced the cost of car, may be credited for start of the lean movement. The introduction of Model T revolutionised the automobile industry by making cars affordable. All new cars were black and Henry Ford's famous statement "Any customer can have a car painted in any colour that he wants so long as it is black" sums up the mass production philosophy of high volumes and negligible variety. Kiichiro Toyoda and Taiichi Ohno of Toyota improved on Ford's approach and developed the Toyota Production System, which is essentially Lean Management. This was popularized by Jim Womack, author of Lean Thinking, The Machine that Changed the World and Lean Solutions.

"All we are doing is looking at the Timeline from the moment customer gives us an order to the point when we collect cash. We are reducing that time line by removing the non-value-added wastes." …Taiichi Ohno.

Lean means eliminating Waste. It is a systematic approach to identifying and eliminating waste (non-value-added activities) through continuous improvement by flowing the product through various processes based on a signal from the customer. Every Process has a Value adding element and a Waste element.

Lean management consists of proven tools and techniques that focus on minimizing wasteful activity and adding value to the product to meet customer needs. The 8 areas of waste can be used to understand the inefficiencies.

① Overproduction	⑤ Inventory
② Extra processing	⑥ Waiting
③ Unnecessary transport	⑦ Defects
④ Unnecessary motion	⑧ Unused employee creativity

Going lean means examining the business processes, identifying waste, focusing on minimizing unnecessary costs, reducing waste and improving inefficient procedures. The benefits are identification of problem areas and bottlenecks, low cost – by eliminating or reducing time on non-value-added activities and increasing productivity.

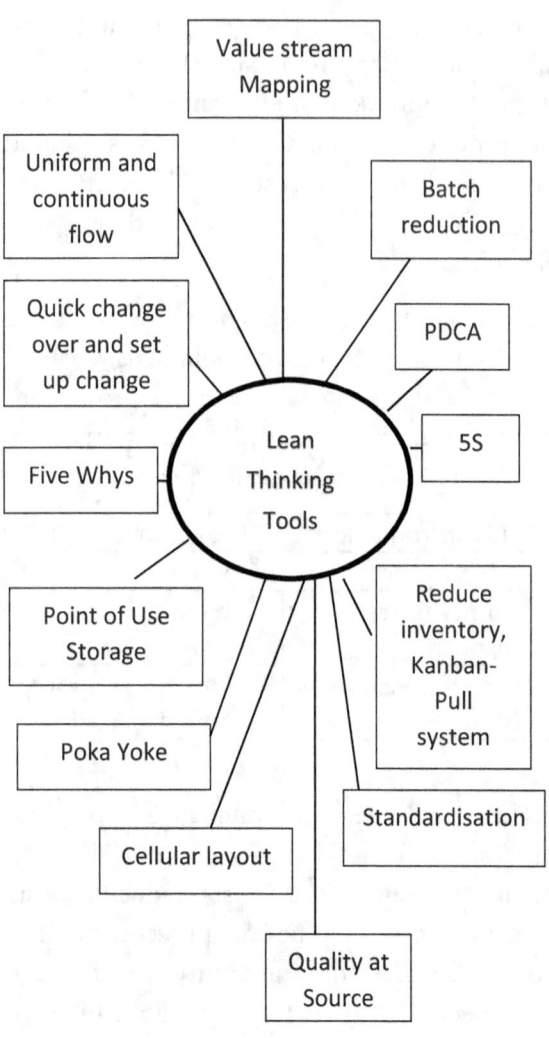

43
JIT

JIT is a system for high-volume production with minimal inventory (raw materials, work in progress, finished goods) and involves timed arrivals at work station, reduction of buffer stocks, producing as per demand and having no waste in the entire supply chain. By reducing inventory, it removes the security blanket and brings to surface the hidden problems of production, maintenance, equipment health, vendor related problems, purchase systems and procedures, process problems, quality problems, people problems etc. Inventory hides problems, JIT exposes them.

The JIT approach helps in finding solutions to following types of problems:

- Lead time is excessive in the entire supply chain: Reducing lead time of suppliers, reducing cycle time, reducing set up and changeover time, reducing transportation time, improving logistics.
- Inventory is high in transit, in stores for materials, in warehouse for finished goods, in

plant and conveyors as work in progress: increasing frequency of deliveries, going for standard packing size, smaller packings, developing vendors nearby, locating operations near to customer, producing on demand, improving processes and equipment health to reduce breakdowns and stoppages, reducing batch sizes, going for line layout.

JIT philosophy is to build a system whose goal is to optimize processes and procedures by continuously pursuing waste reduction, producing only what is needed, when needed.

Basic elements of JIT:

- Pull (Kanban) production control system- Produce what is needed, when it is needed.
- Uniform levelled production flow and streamlined flow.
- Small lot production, faster throughput, greater flexibility.
- Quick set ups and changeovers. This facilitates economical, small lot-size production.
- Flexible manufacturing system (for example, using programmable CNC machines) which makes large variety, small volume feasible.

- Line layout, cellular layout, for higher efficiency.
- Quality at source. Improving quality at source-at supplier end, quality of inputs, equipment settings, process parameters etc- allows zero defect output. Inventory during the process increases due to defectives being generated throughout the line, which necessitates keeping of buffers between work stations. Good quality production facilitates removal of buffers and contributes to the stability of the system.
- Total productive maintenance. Buffers are kept to take care of lost output during equipment stoppages and breakdowns. TPM improves the health of equipment and consequently the stability of the system and reduction of buffers.
- Supplier networks and reliability. As the suppliers do not deliver as per promise or have long delivery times, the manufacturer is forced to keep inventories to enable smooth and uninterrupted production. Having few (one to three) committed and reliable suppliers is better than having multiple vendors. They facilitate small lot delivery, frequent delivery and always on time as per the plan.

Buffer stocks put you in the comfort zone and do not force you to remove the root cause of the problem. The problem remains unresolved till one takes the step of eliminating or reducing inventories.

Inventory Hides Problems, JIT exposes problems, which can then be Solved.			
Unreliable supplier	Rework	Delays	Defects
Logistic constraint	Bad design	Bad layout	Breakdowns
Long lead times	Long change over time	Waiting for material	Long cycle times
Bureaucratic delays	Long set up time	Bad method	Process delays

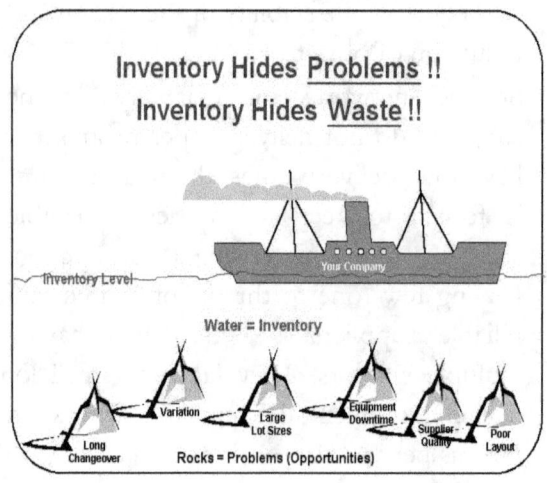

44
Kanban

KANBAN means a 'visible card'. It is a PULL method of controlling materials through a JIT manufacturing assembly by using cards to authorize a workstation to transfer or produce materials. The MRP (Material Requirement Planning) is a PUSH system where material is pushed into the production line based on material requirement as forecasted. In the PULL system, material is moved as per customer demand. No inventory is moved unless authorized by a 'move' card. Each bin contains a fixed, exact quantity of inventory, no more, no less. The 'card' can be paper card or electronic signal.

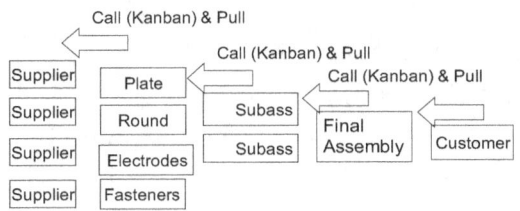

For each bin, there is exactly ONE Kanban card. As soon as materials are removed from a bin, the Kanban card is removed from the bin and placed in move card box. If the bins are not removed by the subsequent process, the operator stops production. This way inventory is controlled.

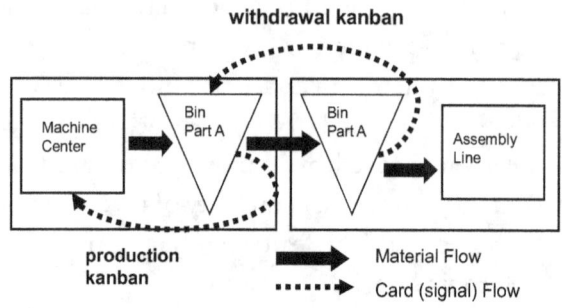

Number of Kanbans N:
$$N = [DL(1+\alpha)]/A$$
Where D=demand per unit of time, L=lead time, A =container capacity, α= safety stock factor.

Kanban		
Part no.	522	
Description	Ball bearings 6204	
	Box Capacity	10
	Supplier	SKF
	Material Issue ref	018
From		**To**
Stores Shed 1		Assembly A-1

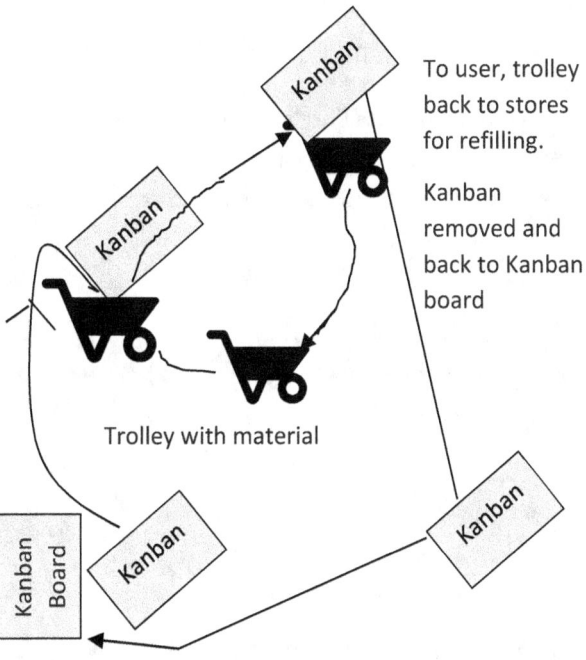

<Exercise>

A switch is assembled in batches of 4 units at an "upstream" work area, delivered in a bin to a "downstream" control-panel assembly area that requires 5 switch assemblies/hour. The switch assembly area can produce a bin of switch assemblies in 2 hours. Safety stock = 10% of needed inventory.

No. of Kanbans
= (Expected demand during lead time + Safety stock)/Container size
= $dL(1+S)/C = 5*2*1.1/4 = 2.75$ or 3 Kanbans

Kanban squares-The item is moved to the next station only if a vacant square is available. Else the line stops, and the team starts working on the problem.

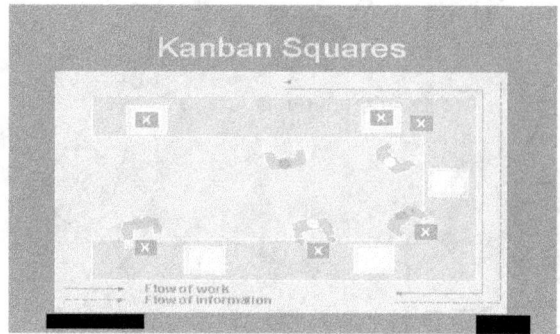

45
TPM

TPM or Total Productive Maintenance is an effective approach applying continuous improvement methods to reduce losses in equipment intensive organisations, be it manufacturing or service. It was started in 1971 by JIPM (Japan Institute of Plant Maintenance) and is an integration of past maintenance activities of Preventive Maintenance with Corrective Maintenance, Predictive Maintenance and Maintenance Prevention, covering the overall life cycle of the equipment, with total employee participation. The objective is to maximise the overall equipment effectiveness (OEE).

TPM philosophy inverts the common understanding that machines cause breakdowns, and that breakdowns will happen, by making people responsible for breakdowns and keeping the breakdown targets as zero. Machines do not break down on their own. The causes are invariably poor design; poor maintenance-lack of routine care like cleaning, oiling, tightening nuts and bolts, irregular daily maintenance and planned maintenance-time based preventive maintenance and condition based predictive maintenance; improper operation practices, lack of skill and training of people using the machine.

A major stumbling block is the mindset and unwillingness to take 'ownership of the equipment' particularly when it is not one's personal asset. The typical mindset, and in many parts of our country a feudal mindset, becomes a big constraint, like "I will not clean," "I am not in maintenance, just a user," "I cannot be responsible for equipment," "It is always done like this here." "Nothing will change here," "First teach the bosses." "I am good, others are the problem," "It can't be done." This must change to 'My equipment,' 'I must look after my equipment' kind of mindset, so that daily care and task of cleaning, oiling, inspection and tightening is done as a habit.

The concept of preventive maintenance is analogous to preventive medicine for keeping a healthy body. Just like the doctor recommends daily prevention, health check ups and early treatment should anything look abnormal, the maintenance manager does daily maintenance to prevent deterioration, measures it and takes preventive steps, and carries out part replacement and repairs where necessary.

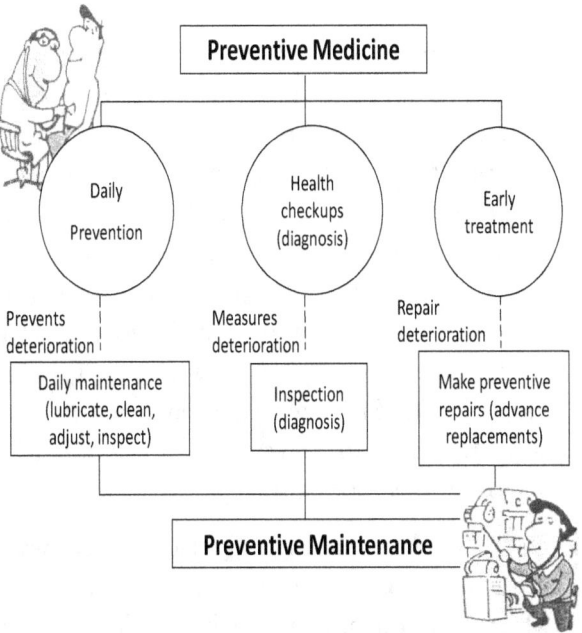

Breakdown attracts breakdown. For example, loose bolt causes vibrations at a certain place, which gradually gives rise to vibrations in other areas and causes failure of all bolts. Lack of oiling enhances friction and increases wear. Lack of cleaning causes dirt, moisture, foreign material to create sludge and force deterioration.

The Stage 1 of breakdown starts with potential minor defects, which initially are hidden, and therefore ignored. In Stage 2, the minor defects become visible like paint peeling off from a small area of the car's body. Stage 3 results in drop in efficiency, performance or aesthetics in a small way. The area, where paint has peeled off, starts rusting and corrosion starts from that point. Stage 4 is when short stoppages occur, and Stage 5 is complete breakdown. The whole car body is corroded, and the car has to go to denting and painting shop for repairs. Another example would be collection of salts inside water pipes because the water quality is bad (high TDS), which subsequently narrows flow cross section, creating pressure drop and stoppage of equipment.

The problem of sudden and major breakdowns is easier to solve as there is a clear cause and effect relationship in such incidents. For example, the car not starting in winter morning because the battery is down as its life is over, and the countermeasure is to replace it with a new battery. However, when the stoppages are chronic, causing small losses and repeating frequently, the solutions are more challenging as the causal relationship is ambiguous. Reducing breakdowns from 10% to 1% is relatively easy, but to reduce it to zero requires innovative solutions.

The Eight Pillars of TPM

TPM

- Improvement
- Planned Maintenance
- Autonomous Maintenance
- Safety, Health, Environment
- Education & Training
- Quality Maintenance
- Development Management
- Office TPM

The objective of TPM is to reduce the **16 major losses** categorised as under:

Seven major losses that can impede equipment efficiency
1. Breakdown/ Failure loss
2. Set up/ adjustment loss
3. Tool/cutting blade loss
4. Start-up loss
5. Minor stoppage loss
6. Speed loss
7. Defect/rework loss

Loss that can impede machine loading time
8. Shutdown loss

Five major losses that can impede improvement of human work efficiency
9. Management loss
10. Motion loss
11. Line organisation loss
12. Loss resulting from failure to automate
13. Measuring and adjustment loss

Three major losses that can impede effective use of production resources
14. Yield loss
15. Energy loss
16. Die, jig, tool loss

Overall Equipment Effectiveness-OEE

OEE = Availability X Performance Rate X Quality Rate

Availability = (Operating or Running time)/(Available or Loading time)

Available (or Loading) Time = Total Time (in shift, or day) – Planned Stoppage time

Operating (or Running) Time = Available (or Loading Time) – Downtime (Failures, set ups)

Availability (Operating Rate) can be improved by eliminating breakdowns, reducing set-ups, adjustment and stoppage losses.

Performance Rate = Actual Output/Standard Output

Performance Rate can be increased by eliminating speed losses, idling and minor stoppages. Actual output would be less than standard output because of reduced speed and minor stoppages.

Quality Rate = Good Output/Actual Output

Quality Rate can be enhanced by eliminating quality defects in the process and during start up. Good output is less than actual output because of scrap, rejections and defectives.

Abnormalities can be identified using the five senses:

Touch-feeling, like touching components to measure vibration, feeling air flow, pressure, surface finish, hair crack.

Eye-see, like observing leaks, spills, adjustments, items lying scattered in work area like operating tools, measuring instruments etc, visual indicator of fumes, air flow, items missing, damaged bolts.

Nose-smell, like burning smell, rotting smell, smoke, dangerous gases, moisture smell etc

Ear-hear, like bearing defects, gear defects, electrical arcing, pressure leaks, minor explosions.

Tongue-Taste, is useful in food and beverages industry like tasting tea, tasting food, chocolates etc.

Decision Making and Implementation

46
Decision Making

A decision is required when there are options, choices and alternatives to choose from. Having no choice, makes decision making easier. When we are solving a problem, effort should be to generate as many solutions to the problem as we can think of. Various problem-solving methods and tools will aid creation of different countermeasures. They must be evaluated and then a decision has to be taken. Decision making is the selection from among alternatives of a course of action.

Decisions can be for routine problems, urgent problems, and difficult or chronic problems. The chronic problems are the most complex and difficult to solve.

Decisions must be arrived at by conscious and diligent approach, which must be transparent, and all concerned should know how decisions are made. However, once the decision is reached, it must be executed with speed. Dragging over a decision forever or procrastinating it will not help.

Decision making authority should be clear. When it is unclear, jointly decide how to decide using your communication and presentation skills.

Steps of decision making

1. Identification and Formulation of problem.
2. Goals to be attained.
3. Boundaries of decision making process.
4. Constraints and assumptions.
5. Development of Alternatives.
6. Measuring the benefits and costs of each alternative.
7. Evaluation of alternatives
8. Selection of the optimal alternative
9. Implementation
10. Checking results of decision with the planned objective.
11. Using above as feedback for further improvement
12. Measures to prevent recurrence of problem

Decision making styles

Autocratic-command based	Decisions are made without involving others. Works for routine problems but may not for complex, and difficult problems. The leader takes the decision and others follow it.
Consultative	All are involved in problem solving, providing inputs, giving ideas and solutions. The final decision is taken by the leader after consultation.
Participative	This is for difficult problems. The leader is part of the group. The decision evolves out of group participation.
Vote based	The majority view point swings the decision.
Consensus	Everyone comes to an agreement and supports the final decision. The disagreement during problem-solving sessions is limited to the sessions, and the participants concur with the final decision taken by the leader.

47
Evaluating Solutions

First provide a screen to filter the options that provide solutions which fulfils the objectives set during problem definition phase. Select top 5 solutions, keeping in mind the barriers and drivers that will restrict or aid you in reaching the desired state.

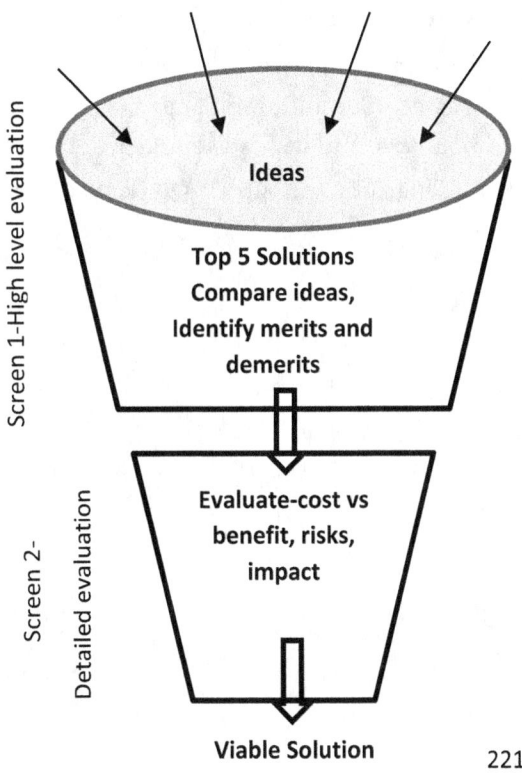

Ask yourself the following questions?

- Did the solution meet the criteria for success?
- What worked? Key learning from it.
- What did not work? Key learning from it.
- What were the constraints to problem solving?
- What should be improved for future problem solving?
- What should be documented?
- Were the deadlines met?
- Was the working in collaboration?
- Was communication among the group members, and with stakeholders, effective?
- How far was the gap closed between actual and desired state?

Weighted Criteria Matrix

The matrix is used when one wants to evaluate objectively how each possible solution meets the set criteria for success. The weights can be from 5 to 1 (5 being most important). The scoring will depend on how well the option meets the criteria with 5 meeting it fully and 1 being non-fulfilment.

Options	Criteria				Total weighted score	Ranking
	Cost	Quality	Speed	User friendly		
Option A						
Weight	4	5	2	3		
Score	3	2	4	5		
Weighted score	12	10	8	15	45	2
Option B						
Weight	4	5	2	3		
Score	4	5	4	4		
Weighted score	16	25	8	12	61	1
Option C						
Weight	4	5	2	3		
Score	2	3	1	4		
Weighted score	8	15	2	12	37	3

Option B is the best solution.

Risk Assessment

After narrowing down the options to a few solutions, one can evaluate the degree of manageable risks associated with possible actions and solutions.

List the risks and the probability the risk will occur (1 being most probable and 5 being the most). Assess the seriousness of impact of each risk (1 being least impactful, 5 being the most). The risk potential is computed by adding the number in the probability and the impact columns. Then write the contingency plan (or action plan) for managing each risk, and the person or team responsible for the contingency plan.

Risk	Impact of risk	Probability	Risk Score (weight)	Avoidance	Responsibility
Type of risk	Scale 1 to 5	Scale 1 to 5	Total	Contingency Plan	Person/team

48

Implementation

No organisation or person can deliver on its commitments unless the discipline of execution is practised. Execution is the missing link between aspirations and results.

To be good in execution, you have to be where the action is, set clear goals and priorities, recognise and reward the doers, and develop the capability of your team.

Key components for driving a successful implementation plan:

1. Define actionable goals
2. Prepare actionable plan-list tasks, define predecessors, set timelines, schedule milestones. Use Gantt chart, network techniques (PERT/CPM) and project management resources.
3. Allocate resources-people, time, money, equipments, materials
4. Assign roles and responsibility-involve correct people at correct times, have strong team leader, and shared vision.
5. Define metrics for measuring progress and successful implementation.

6. Contingency planning-consider factors which can go wrong.
7. Continual monitoring and reviews to evaluate incremental success and progress, celebrate achievements, quality communication among people, publicising plan and its progress, making work visible to get people engagement and motivate, inspire others.

Action Plan

Goals and Desired Outcomes	Action Steps	Responsibility	Start date	End date	Status
Goal 1					
Write your goal statement					
List Resources					
Desired Outcome					
Goal 2					
Write your goal statement					
List Resources					
Desired Outcome					
Goal 3					
Write your goal statement					
List Resources					
Desired Outcome					

Problem Solving Competencies

49
Holistic Thinking

Psychologists and scientists have observed that problem solving becomes more effective when all the four quadrants of the brain are used for thinking.

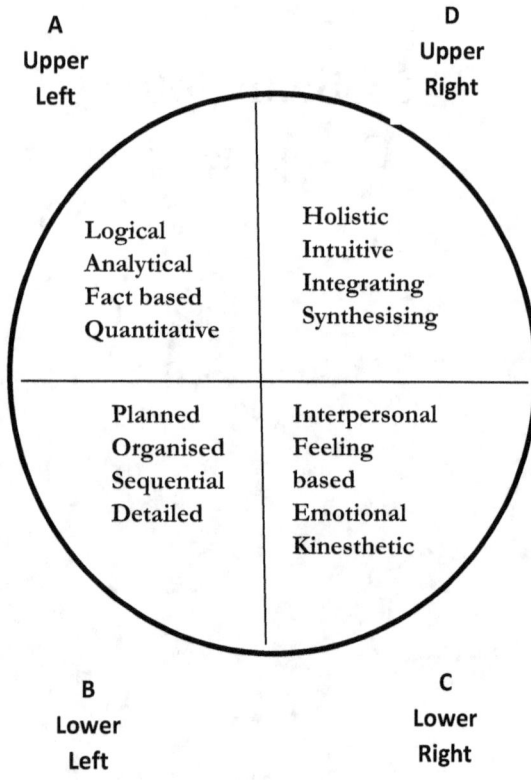

Quadrant A: Rational and Analytical Self	
At School	Maths, Science, Computers
At Work	Engineer, Finance
Decision Making	Rational, facts based
Problem solving	Logical, makes models, forms theories, measures precisely
Hobbies	Computer games, model making, home improvements

Quadrant B: Organised and Planning Self	
At School	Language, Geography, History
At Work	Manager, Project management
Decision Making	Procedural, firm, conservative
Problem solving	Practical approach to problems
Hobbies	Reading, Golf, Travel, Spectator sports

Quadrant C: Emotional and Feeling Self	
At School	Drama, Literature, Social science
At Work	Social worker, trainer, teacher
Decision Making	Emotional, Intuitive, involves others, interpersonal
Problem solving	Considers others, Takes non-verbal and interpersonal cues, intuitive
Hobbies	Music, walking, relaxing, travel

Quadrant D: Creative and Experimental Self	
At School	Science, Maths, Arts & Crafts
At Work	Self-employed, entrepreneur, Designer
Decision Making	Imaginative, risk taking, forward looking
Problem solving	Sees the big picture, inventive, intuitive
Hobbies	Creative writing, Music playing, photography, Arts & Crafts

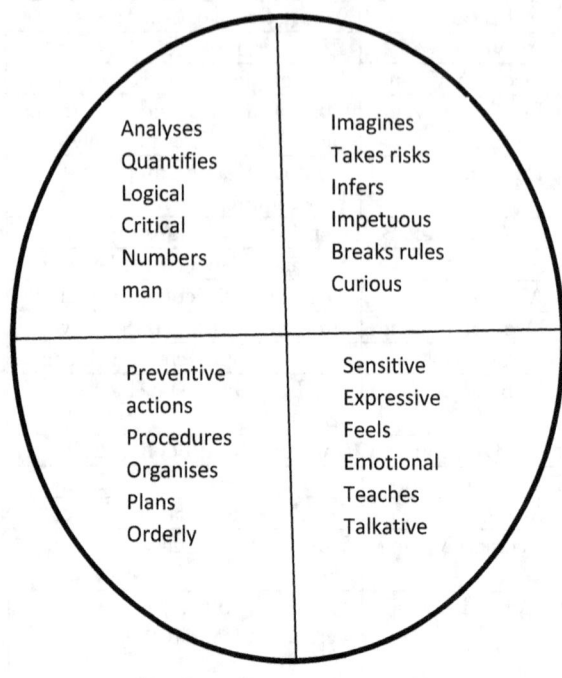

Whole Brain Thinking

50
Competencies

Problem solving requires the ability to identify and formulate the problem, develop and implement solutions, using creative and analytical approaches, that effectively and quickly resolve the concerned problem.

One needs to develop following skills for problem solving:

1. Critical thinking-objective analysis of facts and data to form a judgment and develop integrated solutions. Critical thinking is self-motivated, self-disciplined and self-corrective thinking. "Socratic Questioning" is the best example of critical thinking strategy. Critical thinking is logical, analytical, complex reasoning, creative and empathetic thinking, which questions the status quo, challenges the existing way of thinking and doing things, and solves ambiguous problems.

2. Root cause analysis-identifies causal links to the problem and the root cause, which helps in troubleshooting and leads to generation of solutions to eliminate the problem. Probes issues to get to the root of a problem.

3. Technical grasp of the problem- multi-disciplinary knowledge and skills to understand the problem and current situation holistically.

4. External perspective- Embraces differing views for thorough examination before acting.

5. Decision making, risk taking and Execution-develops several alternative solutions to problem, weighs pros and cons, evaluates risks against benefits, decides and implements.

6. Interpersonal skills and team work

7. Communication and presentation skills to get the support and sponsorship (for larger problems) of the stakeholders.

8. Leadership-to energise and motivate the team.

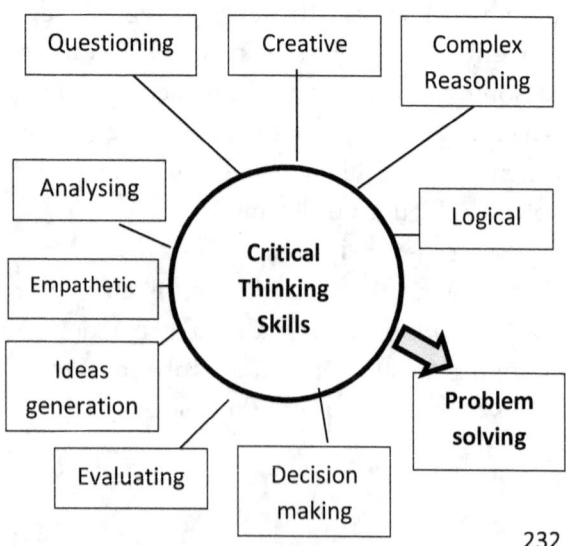

Competency Levels		
Level	Competency	
1	Foundational	Sees relationship between current and past solved problems
2	Experienced	Uses creative and analytical approaches to solve problems. Goes beyond immediately presented information. Probes deeper to get to the root of the problem.
3	Advanced	Solves multi-dimensional and multi-functional problems. Gathers information over an extended period of time and applies complex concepts or methods to generate solutions.
4	Expert	Solves ambiguous problems-analyses complex problems involving multiple variables, their relationships and interactions, when data is amorphous and incomplete, or missing.

Developing Self

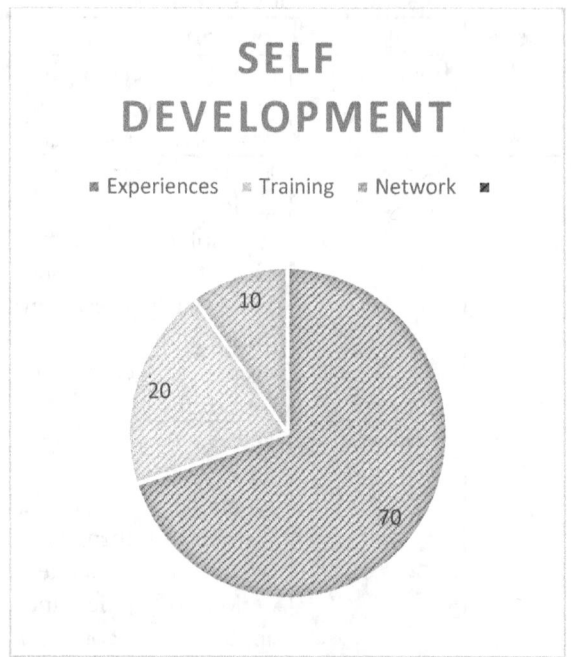

Experiences -70% of learning is on the job. To gain problem solving experience, undertake challenging assignments with difficult and stretched goals, grab opportunities in cross functional and global projects, look for leadership roles, and volunteer to participate in problem solving events like Kaizen, QC circles, suggestion schemes etc. One can also gain experience by job shadowing, and knowledge sharing through knowledge bank.

Network-20% of learning is through other people, feedback, networking, mentoring, coaching and participating in communities.

Training -10% of learning is through OJT (on the job training) and classroom training, workshops, and self-study. Training can be offline or online through the medium of WhatsApp, Skype, web seminar, video conferencing etc.

Bibliography

1. The Toyota Way by Jeffrey K Liker
2. The Six Sigma Way by Peter S. Pande, Robert P. Neuman, Roland R. Cavanagh
3. Kaizen by Masaaki Imai
4. Statistics for Management by Richard I. Levin and David S. Rubin
5. Fortune at the bottom of the pyramid by C. K. Prahalad
6. Total Quality Management, John S. Oakland
7. Management by Quality, Hitoshi Kume
8. Theory of constraints by Eliyahu M. Goldratt
9. The Goal by Eliyahu M. Goldratt
10. Three box solution by Vijay Govindrajan
11. Execution By Larry Bossidy & Ram Charan
12. Putting your company's whole brain to work-Harvard Business Review, July 1997
13. Six thinking hats by Edward de Bono
14. Lateral thinking by Edward de Bono
15. Zero Quality Control: Source Inspection and the Poka Yoke System by Shigeo Shingo
16. Statistical Quality Control by Eugene L. Grant
17. Reengineering the corporation by Michael Hammer
18. Problem Solving 101 by Ken Watanabe

19. The Thinker's Toolkit by Morgan D. Jones
20. Straight from the guts by Jack Welch
21. The Creative Problem Solver, Ian Atkinson
22. The IBM way by Buck Rodgers
23. IACOCCA, an autobiography by Lee Iacocca
24. What they don't teach you at Harvard Business School by Mark H. McCormack
25. Total Quality Management by Besterfield
26. Juran's Quality Handbook, Joseph M. Juran
27. The Six Sigma Handbook, Thomas Pyzdek
28. Project Management, Eric Larson and Clifford Gray
29. Management for Quality Improvement: The 7 New QC tools by Sigeru Mizuno
30. Lean Thinking by P. James Womack
31. TPM in process industries by Tokutaro Suzuki
32. Asking the Right Questions by Neil Browne
33. Critical Thinking by Linda Elder and Richard W. Paul
34. Mind Map by Tony Buzan
35. TRIZ by K.Ganapathy, P.V.satyavratan, Quality Circle Forum of India
36. Quality is free by Philip B Crosby
37. Made in Japan, Akio Morita and SONY
38. Toyota Culture, Jeffrey K. Liker

About J.M.Pant
Mentor, Trainer and Founder-NGO

Jitendra .M. Pant is a seasoned and distinguished mentor, life coach, and trainer, specialising in personal and professional transformation, with a versatile skill set honed through extensive experience in Operations Management. His areas of work cover Operations Excellence, Total Productivity and Quality Management, 5S, Kaizen, QC tools, TPM, Problem solving, Six sigma, Project Management, Supply Chain Management, Entrepreneurship, Business and Operations Strategy for MSME units, Soft Skills, and People Development He has been very effective in coaching owners of small and medium size organisations and institutions.

An avid lifelong learner with over 45 years of rich, non-linear career, he has been deeply engaged in various sectors of manufacturing industry, services, consultancy and education.

In his senior citizen years, driven by a spirit of service and altruism, Jitendra.M.Pant founded the JMPS Health & Education Care Foundation, registered as a section 8 company.

His versatility, interdisciplinary experience, and a solid foundation in technical learning are exemplified by his academic journey, having earned both B. Tech and M. Tech degrees from the prestigious IIT Delhi.

He has done overseas assignments in Japan, South Korea, England, Scotland, Kenya, and has widely travelled in India and abroad for work, personal learning, exploration and self-discovery. He is author of books on 5S, Time Management, Confidence building, 25 lessons from uncommon thoughts, No, Problem solving, Wisdom in Verses, Nano Insights and Operations Management Demystified. He runs an online course in Udemy on 5S. Books are available on pothi.com, amazon.in, flipkart.com and amazon.com.

Contact : jm.pant@gmail.com; +919811030273
www.jmpshealthedu.co.in

www.ingramcontent.com/pod-product-compliance
Lightning Source LLC
Chambersburg PA
CBHW071826210526
45479CB00001B/15